FRANK LLOYD WRIGHT'S
FALLINGWATER

The House and Its History

by DONALD HOFFMANN

With an Introduction by
Edgar Kaufmann, jr.

DOVER PUBLICATIONS, INC.
NEW YORK

Published in Canada by General Publishing
Company, Ltd., 30 Lesmill Road, Don Mills,
Toronto, Ontario.
Published in the United Kingdom by Constable
and Company, Ltd., 10 Orange Street, London
WC2H 7EG.

*Frank Lloyd Wright's Fallingwater: The House
and Its History* is a new work, first published by
Dover Publications, Inc., in 1978, by special
arrangement with the Western Pennsylvania Conservancy, Pittsburgh.

International Standard Book Number:
0-486-23671-4
Library of Congress Catalog Card Number:
77-81471

Manufactured in the United States of America
Dover Publications, Inc.
180 Varick Inc.
New York, N.Y. 10014

ACKNOWLEDGMENTS

About any great work of art it is hardly possible to learn as much as one would like to know. This narrative could not have been written without the help of many persons who were willing to share their knowledge, their memories and their interest. I must thank Byron Keeler Mosher, Edgar Tafel, Abrom Dombar, John H. Howe, Blaine Drake, John Lautner, Robert F. Bishop and William Wesley Peters, who were among the earliest members of the Taliesin Fellowship, and two later members, Robert Warn and especially Curtis Besinger. I am also indebted to Lloyd Wright, Mrs. Mendel Glickman, Paul Grotz, Henry Wright, George Nelson, Lewis Mumford, Robert Kostka, John McAndrew, Robert Mark, J. O. Hedrich, Harold Corsini, Oliver M. Kaufmann, E. S. Colborn, Paul L. Cvecko, Walter W. Getzel, William E. Edmunds, William R. Upthegrove, Murlin R. Hodgell, Richard Hollander, Alan Hoffmann, William H. Sims, Gary S. Smith, Roger Kraft and E. Eugene Young. And to the members of the administrative staff at Bear Run and in the offices of the Western Pennsylvania Conservancy: Edward A. Robinson, Earl Friend, Thomas M. Schmidt, Joshua C. Whetzel, jr., Bill Randour and Paul G. Wiegman. Adolf K. Placzek, Avery Librarian at Columbia University, was unfailingly courteous and helpful. I am also grateful to Brendan Gill for his interest. The project was initiated by Edgar Kaufmann, jr., who encouraged it and informed it; and most of all I am grateful to him.

D. H.

VISITING THE HOUSE

Fallingwater is now a property of the Western Pennsylvania Conservancy. Tours are conducted from the first Tuesday in April until mid-November. For further details and reservations, call Fallingwater, Mill Run, Pennsylvania, 412/329-8501.

INTRODUCTION

Fallingwater has provided enjoyment to many people over the years; as a stimulating weekend retreat for the Kaufmann family and their friends, as a source of pride to the architect and his associates, and now—cared for by the Western Pennsylvania Conservancy—as an exceptional experience for visitors from near and far. These varied groups of people have one thing in common, the appreciation of nature. Fallingwater brings people and nature together in an easy relationship; that is the source of its great appeal, of its worldwide fame as one of Frank Lloyd Wright's masterworks. Now, however, country houses so extensive and demanding of services are hardly workable. As a result, has Fallingwater become no more than a delightful relic? No, together with its setting the house illustrates fundamental concepts applicable to different circumstances. The passage of time has brought Fallingwater unanticipated opportunities, and Wright's architecture responds readily.

When Wright came to the site he appreciated the powerful sound of the falls, the vitality of the young forest, the dramatic rock ledges and boulders; these were elements to be interwoven with the serenely soaring spaces of his structure. But Wright's insight penetrated more deeply. He understood that people were creatures of nature, hence an architecture which conformed to nature would conform to what was basic in people. For example, although all of Fallingwater is opened by broad bands of windows, people inside are sheltered as in a deep cave, secure in the sense of hill behind them. Their attention is directed toward the outside by low ceilings; no lordly hall sets the tone but, instead, the luminous textures of the woodland, rhythmically enframed. The materials of the structure blend with the colorings of rocks and trees, while occasional accents are provided by bright furnishings, like the wildflowers or birds outside. The paths within the house, stairs and passages, meander without formality or urgency, and the house hardly has a main entrance; there are many ways in and out. Sociability and privacy are both available, as are the comforts of home and the adventures of the seasons. So people are cosseted into relaxing, into exploring the enjoyment of a life refreshed in nature. Visitors, too, in due measure experience Wright's architecture as an expansion of living.

The interplay of people and nature does not depend on any one architectural expression, it is a point of view which can be ever freshly manifested. Fallingwater speaks eloquently for this point of view. It indicates a world in which the works of mankind and the processes of nature harmonize productively. Thus it upholds the spirit and purpose of the Western Pennsylvania Conservancy in making nature known as a vital, irreplaceable source of human values.

This book of Donald Hoffmann's, based on his careful research, tells how the house came into being. With delightful fidelity it evokes the volatile but crucial relationship between Wright and my father, and it divulges the complex practicalities of realizing a genial, innovative design. Hoffmann has written a true architectural record, a rare and wonderful accomplishment. Brendan Gill helped unselfishly to make the book a reality. To all concerned with it I express cordial appreciation.

EDGAR KAUFMANN, JR.

February 1977

CONTENTS

LIST OF ILLUSTRATIONS

FRANK LLOYD WRIGHT'S
FALLINGWATER
The House and Its History

1. *Bear Run, Fayette County, Pa.*

2. *Mountain ridge above Bear Run.*

Chapter I
BEAR RUN

Of course the stream itself, which is called Bear Run, came first [Fig. 1]. Slight and swift and not very easy to find, Bear Run is fed by mountain springs, and its entire course is only four miles. It flickers down the western slopes of the ridge called Laurel Hill to join the Youghiogheny River, and it moves fast because it falls from about 2500 feet above sea level to about 1070 feet [2]. Bear Run is only a stream, not a town. It is not well represented on any map of less detail, or lesser scale, than the Mill Run Quadrangle topographic map, as edited and published by the U.S. Geological Survey [3]. There are many other runs, or small fast streams, in Stewart Township and in Fayette County, and altogether too many to count in the rest of southwestern Pennsylvania and throughout the Appalachians.

And so Bear Run is both obscure and unexceptional, or so it might have been. But at a place where it flows at 1298 feet above sea level, then breaks to fall about 20 feet, a house was built from plans by Frank Lloyd Wright [4]. He called it "Fallingwater." The owners, who were Mr. and Mrs. Edgar J. Kaufmann of Pittsburgh, more easily thought of their new weekend house simply as "Bear Run," because the place had already been their retreat for some 15 years. By whatever name, and from the day in September 1935 when Wright first sketched it, the house was so surely the work of an extraordinary imagination, so radiant and right for its time and forest place, that it seemed certain to become

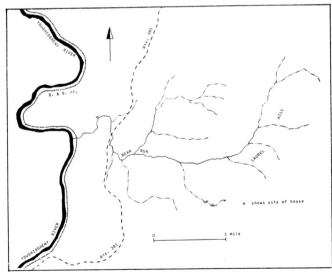

3. Map of Bear Run.

4. Waterfall on Bear Run, before 1912.

5. Fallingwater.

one of the most celebrated houses of our century [5]. And it very soon did.

The house on Bear Run stands today as a most remarkable work of art. Many questions can easily be asked about it; some, perhaps, can be answered now. What is the nature of Bear Run? Who was there first, and why? When did the Kaufmanns learn of Bear Run? When did they build their first weekend house there? Why did they want a new house? When did they talk to Wright about it? What could Wright have noticed when he first saw Bear Run? How did he conceive the house? How was it built?

Of the stream itself there is little record, for nature exists so easily without man and writes its story, if at all, not in man's language. It is hardly apparent, for instance, that in the very long period from 600 million to 425 million years ago all of western Pennsylvania was merely part of a vast and shallow sea. But geology tells us that much; and also that the crust of the earth, through a most tedious contest between the sea and a continental land mass, which bordered the southeast corner of Pennsylvania, was layered with sedimentary deposits: the muds, sands and shells that changed so slowly into shales, sandstones and limestones. The strata became thousands of feet deep, and at first they lay almost horizontally; but some unknown and awesome force within the earth, radiating from the southeast, buckled and arched the rock into parallel open folds. The process, we are told, began about 230 million years ago. It continued to wrench and twist the rock at an inconceivably slow pace. Erosion wore down the rock and filled the valleys. Dinosaurs foraged in the swamps until they finally disappeared, some 65 million years ago. About 50 million years ago, the plain began to rise: another great force was at work, and it formed the Allegheny Plateau. As the land rose higher the streams fell farther, thus flowed faster. They cut deeper channels, then opened the valleys, and very slowly laid bare the ancient rock folds, mountains older than the Rockies and much older than the Alps. The ripple of ridges and valleys across most of Pennsylvania, from southwest to northeast, bears witness to that immense deformation of the earth.

Bear Run flows into the Ohiopyle Valley, framed by the traces of the ancient mountains: to the east, Laurel Hill, and to the west, Chestnut Ridge. The land near the waterfalls consists of dense and heavy-bedded sandstones of the Pottsville formation, some dark gray and some buff-colored. From weakness came beauty. When the stream worked away at a flawed joint in the rock it finally fractured; parts of the rock crashed down to rest as huge boulders [6], and Bear Run broke over falls.[1] The cascade—all along Bear Run there are many smaller falls—became central to Wright's conception of the

6. *Boulders below falls, before 1912.*

house; the dark boulders on the north side of the stream were crucial to the way in which he sited it; and the buff-colored sandstone ledges, which cropped out here and there along the stream, became one more key to its character.

The first Americans in western Pennsylvania were the Indians, who, at least 16,000 years ago and probably a few thousand years earlier, crossed the land to hunt and fish. Because of their relatively gentle ways, they left hardly a trace, only a few buried bones and artifacts. British troops, in the later 1750s, reported signs of Indians a

[1] For a diagram of the typical rock-structure pattern in Stewart Township, see W. O. Hickok IV and F. T. Moyer, *Geology and Mineral Resources of Fayette County Pennsylvania* (Harrisburg, Pa., 1940), fig. 113—although the relation of the rock beds is now thought to be even more complex, with interbeddings from different ages. Glaciers crossed parts of northern Pennsylvania, but did not reach the Ohiopyle Valley. For a general account, see Bradford Willard, *Pennsylvania Geology Summarized* (Harrisburg, Pa., 1962).

7. Rhododendron at Bear Run.

few miles north of the Bear Run falls. The Indians who passed through the valley were from the Delaware, Shawnee and Iroquois tribes and they called it "Ohiopehelle," meaning a white-water place, just as they named the river itself the "Yohoghany," to express its twisted course on the way north to meet the Monongahela.

White settlers reached the valley slowly, toward the end of the eighteenth century. They were mostly of English, German and Irish Protestant origins. Gradually they gathered into a small community three and a half miles north of the falls; at first it was called Bigamtown, but since 1866 it has been known as Mill Run, in recognition of Reuben Skinner's grist mill.[2] Milling in the valley lasted until the 1940s, but it was not one of the principal ways by which the mountain people lived off the land—rarely to the land's advantage, often enough not even to their own. Mining was important and so was timbering. Coal and clay were taken from the hills, and on the Bear

Run grounds even the sandstone was broken up to be sold as "ganister rock," for use in building brick kilns or in making refractory products such as silica brick; in 1920, the rock was bringing 25 cents a ton. The forest was cut over and over again, for posts and mining timbers and railroad ties. Tramways crossed the grounds in conveying the timbers down to the Youghiogheny, where a sawmill stood on a site of more than five acres near the mouth of Bear Run. A few miles up the river, at the village of Ohiopyle, there was a pulp mill.

When the first members of the Kaufmann family in western Pennsylvania picked their way through the sparsely settled mountains to sell cloths and notions, well before the turn of the century, they often encountered trappers; and as late as 1933 a game commissioner could report that fox, mink, weasel and skunk were still being trapped along Bear Run. The stream was fished with a certain singlemindedness: one man boasted in 1880 of having caught 153 trout in a single day's work. Some chose to farm the land, even if the forest and the rocks gave little encouragement; and, as if in repayment to the unyielding nature of the soil, they cared very little about erosion. The mountain people tended to live a frontier life long after the entire American Frontier, so far as historians could tell, had vanished. If today Bear Run looks unspoiled, it is not because the land or the timber is in any sense virgin; just about everything that could have been done there was, in fact, done. Nature with help healed some of its lesser wounds, and the dense forest cover can conceal most of the signs of those unfortunate encounters between man and the land.

What serves Bear Run so well is the richness of its native plant life. Most characteristic is the great laurel, or common rhododendron, which flourishes because of the moisture from the stream, the shade of the taller trees and a soil enriched by fallen oak leaves. In summertime the white blossoms ornament the forest with a fragile beauty; in every season the long smooth leaves stay green [7]. Mountain laurels are intermixed, and so are the oaks and other hardwoods and the little Christmas ferns, descendants of the giant ferns from the ancient era when the coal beds were formed. The trees that grew nearest to the waterfalls when Wright first saw Bear Run included white oak, black oak, red oak, birch, tulip, maple, hickory, butternut, apple and wild black cherry.[3]

[2] See *A History of Mill Run, Fayette County, Pennsylvania* (Mill Run, Pa., 1970). Also see Solon Justus Buck and Elizabeth Hawthorn Buck, *The Planting of Civilization in Western Pennsylvania* (Pittsburgh, Pa., 1939).

[3] All were identified in a contour map requested by Wright and dated March 9, 1935. Also see John F. Lewis, *Guide to Plants, Bear Run Nature Reserve* (Western Pennsylvania Conservancy, Pittsburgh, 1968). Lewis identified 501 species and Frank L. Lowden has found 33 additional species. About 130 kinds of birds have been sighted in recent years, and 20 mammals ranging in size from the tiny woodland jumping mouse to the northern white-tailed deer. Residents of the area say that occasionally a black bear is sighted, but naturalists have yet to encounter one within the nature reserve.

There was no real sign of any care about Bear Run until 1890, when a group of Masons from Pittsburgh bought more than 135 acres of land there from Joseph Soisson, Zachariah Moon and a few other settlers. Not that the Masons were conservationists; but at least they saw in Bear Run a recreational value. They built the "Masonic Country Club," and at first it thrived; in August 1895 they bought about 1500 acres more. But within a decade the club had failed. The property was sold at a sheriff's auction in June 1906, sold again in October 1907 and still again in March 1909, when another Masonic body in Pittsburgh, the Syria Improvement Association, acquired the camp and revived it as the "Syria Country Club."[4] By then there were more than a dozen buildings: the club house, six cottages, a dance pavilion and various outbuildings [8].

It was also in 1909 that Edgar Jonas Kaufmann married Lillian Sarah Kaufmann.[5] They were married in New York City because they could not have been married legally in Pennsylvania; they were first cousins. Kaufmann was the elder son of Morris Kaufmann, and his bride was the daughter of Isaac Kaufmann. Morris and Isaac and two more brothers of theirs, Henry and Jacob, had left Viernheim, in Hessen, Germany, and arrived in western Pennsylvania in the 1860s. They were

tailors and merchants, and very good ones. In 1871, with only 1500 dollars, they opened a store in Pittsburgh, mostly to offer ready-made men's clothing. Their business grew, they moved in 1885 to a building at Fifth Avenue and Smithfield Street, and there Kaufmann's Store has stayed ever since. Traditionally it was known as "The Big Store." Edgar J. Kaufmann was born in 1885, and he grew along with the business. He trained in Germany, in Marshall Field's in Chicago and in a general store in Connellsville, only 16 miles from Bear Run. By 1913, when his father bought Henry Kaufmann's interest in the store and he bought Isaac's—Jacob had died in 1905— Edgar J. Kaufmann took active control of Kaufmann's Store.

Among his papers is a plan of the Bear Run property dated November 1913.[6] It shows the Syria Club House to be sited about 1100 feet southeast of the falls, at an elevation 114 feet higher. It also shows a Bear Run Station on the Baltimore & Ohio Railroad [9], high above the east side of the Youghiogheny River: access to the club grounds from Pittsburgh depended to a large extent on the railroad and the willingness of the engineers to stop on a steep uphill grade. Thirteen other structures (all of them, over the years, have been demolished) are shown on the map. One, identified as the Porter cottage, is on

---

[4] The chain of title to the Bear Run property from 1890 to the present can be traced at the office of the Fayette County Recorder of Deeds, Uniontown, Pa., in deed books 137–139, 146, 261, 291, 321, 379, 406, 471, 472, 519, 535 and 982.

[5] She later changed the spelling of her name to "Liliane."

[6] The Bear Run papers that have survived are now in the special collections of the Avery Architectural Library, Columbia University in the City of New York. They were donated by Edgar Kaufmann, jr. Facts in this narrative not otherwise provided with sources are drawn mostly from those papers.

8. *Syria Country Club House, Bear Run, before 1912.*

9. Mouth of Bear Run. B. & O. tracks at top.

the cliff north of the falls [10], exactly where Wright would site the guest wing of Fallingwater, 26 years later. The road to the Porter cottage crosses a simple wooden truss bridge, east of the falls; a hatchery for brook trout, not far from the bridge, is evidence enough that the native supply already had been depleted.

Whether this plan of 1913, prepared by William Bradford, a Pittsburgh engineer, was drawn at Kaufmann's request is not clear; but in 1916 the merchant established "Kaufmann's Summer Club" on Bear Run as a vacation place for women employees of his store.[7] A club brochure from 1926 describes the activities: tennis, swimming, volleyball, hiking, hayrides, picnicking, sunbathing, singing, theater and "quiet" reading. The club, a retreat from "the heat and turmoil of the city," is 72 miles from Pittsburgh, a train ride of only two hours. The station is the starting point for a climb "up the mountain road lined with mountain laurel and rhododendron to the accompaniment of the gentle roar of the water in Bear Run . . . ." (The station stood at an elevation 260 feet lower than that of the clubhouse. Edgar Kaufmann, jr., remembers it as merely a shelter fashioned from an old freight car with one of its sides removed; an early photograph shows it to have been rather well disguised. The mountain road leading up to the camp was on the south side of the stream, and is still kept clear.)

In the years when the store's summer club leased the camp, the property changed hands again. More than 600 acres were sold in December 1918, for only 20,000 dollars. Early in 1920, 300 acres, including all the improvements, were offered to Kaufmann at 25,000 dollars. He considered the offer cautiously and with a great deal of foresight; he asked Morris Knowles, Inc., a Pittsburgh firm of engineers, to report on the entire site: the topography, water, sewerage and mineral resources. In a report on March 24, 1920, the engineers estimated the value of the improvements alone to be more than 48,000 dollars. But by then only 130 acres were offered for sale. In June the engineers presented a general plan to develop the

[7] Edgar Kaufmann, jr., believes that his father first heard of Bear Run from Charles A. Filson, who was a store detective, a close friend and a Mason, thus presumably aware of the earlier clubs. The idea of a store summer club may have been largely Filson's. He occasionally represented Kaufmann in club matters, and he was one of the club's advisory directors. An employees' organization, the Kaufmann Beneficial and Protective Association, administered the club. The store had its own social-service department in those years; a concern for working women—or what they might be doing when not working—was typical of American cities from the late nineteenth century into the early decades of this century. As late as 1929, the landscape architect Jens Jensen expressed it so: "What do our young people, spending their lives in great buildings, have in their heads? . . . Little except sex! Trees and water and sky have things to tell them which they should hear if their minds are not to become narrow . . ." (*Chicago Daily News*, June 24, 1929, sec. 2, p. 14).

10. Porter cottage and wooden truss bridge, near Bear Run falls, before 1912.

summer club; they recommended to Kaufmann that he buy the entire grounds, especially to prevent contamination of the watershed by coal-mine openings, lumber camps or trespassers.

The negotiations came to nothing. But for the first time there was a clear understanding of the need to conserve Bear Run by gaining control of the watershed. Some of the camp buildings were remodeled and repaired for the 1920 season, and the club took a second five-year lease in 1921. In that same year Kaufmann and his wife built their first weekend house on Bear Run: a modest "Readicut" summer cabin supplied by the Aladdin Company of Bay City, Michigan.[8] They built it 1500 feet southeast of the falls, on a site slightly west of the road between Mill Run and Ohiopyle, at the edge of a cliff; everyone soon took to calling it the "Hangover." The cabin had screened sleeping porches on every side, but had no plumbing, heating or electricity. (Mill Run was not served with electricity until 1928. In preparation for a family celebration of Mrs. Morris Kaufmann's seventieth birthday, in 1931, the Kaufmanns enlarged their cabin by adding a

living room, with a fireplace in what Edgar Kaufmann, jr., remembers as "a hideous rustic-rocky chimney.")

In May 1926, just before the club entered its eleventh season, the store employees' association bought the Bear Run property, 1598 and 7/100 acres. Kaufmann held the mortgage. Gradually, the summer camp lost its appeal; once, because of labor troubles, the employees boycotted it. With the Depression the place fell into disuse. Kaufmann nevertheless continued to regard Bear Run with great affection. When he got a letter in December 1932

8 The company's *Catalog No. 32* (Bay City, 1919–1920), p. 3, explains that the system means that "every bit of work that *can* be done by machine *should* be so done"; the system is compared with the fabrication of steel for skyscrapers. Wright also was intently interested in systems and, between 1912 and 1916, worked on plans for "American System-Built Houses," which were advertised as being "as sound from the engineer's viewpoint as a great bridge or a skyscraper." See *Antonin Raymond: An Autobiography* (Rutland, Vt., 1973), pp. 48–51. Wright's textile-block houses of the 1920s were based on a system of pre-cast concrete blocks joined and reinforced at the site, and in 1937 he designed a series of "All-Steel Houses" for prefabrication. See *Frank Lloyd Wright: Drawings for a Living Architecture* (New York, 1959), pp. 190–194.

from V. M. Bearer, a district forester with the Pennsylvania Department of Forests and Waters, saying that the "old dead chestnuts" should be removed as soon as possible—they were victims of the 1920s chestnut blight—Kaufmann made a note to use the trees for firewood and to build split-rail fences. He had a few of the trunks sawed into sections to serve as rustic coffee tables. Bearer also suggested that the caretaker, Herbert Ohler, might well plant "a few thousands" of Norway spruce in the openings of the forest. Kaufmann had that done too. He must have been pleased when he got a letter in February 1933 from W. L. Wright of the International Association of Game, Fish and Conservation Commissioners, who appraised the grounds as "one of the best ranges for a game preserve that I have ever looked over." In May 1933, Kaufmann corresponded with the Pennsylvania Board of Fish Commissioners about a plan to replenish the brook trout in Bear Run. By the time he and his wife took title to the grounds personally, in July 1933, they were committed to a comprehensive program of conservation. They eventually owned 1914 acres on Bear Run, and the house that Wright was to design for them would serve as one of their homes for many years to come.

Chapter II
THE HOUSE IS CONCEIVED: 1935

There was reason enough by 1934 to assume that Frank Lloyd Wright was well into the twilight years of his long and immensely productive career. He turned 67 years old that June, and, although his home, "Taliesin," south of Spring Green, Wisconsin, was alive with eager apprentices, his architectural practice had shriveled to almost nothing. In the summer of 1932 he planned a house for Malcolm Willey, in Minneapolis; more than a year and a half later he was still at work on drawings of a second scheme for the same house. (And it was not by any means a large house: the first version, Wright estimated, would have cost 16,500 dollars, and the house as built in 1934 cost 10,000). But of course these were the Depression years. Even so, the house for Willey was only the second commission that Wright had seen realized since 1927, and the first was a house for his cousin, Richard Lloyd Jones. Wright was never not busy, as one of his apprentices said not long ago, but at the time—so far as the world outside Taliesin could tell—he was up to very little, beyond his writing and lecturing. The sense of frustration seemed apparent even in the way he wrote: "I would much rather build than write about building," he wrote in 1928, "but when I am not building, I will write about building—or the significance of those buildings I have already built."[1]

From those lean years came *An Autobiography*, the long and episodic narrative in which Wright revealed his emotional depth even more forcefully than the radical nature of his architecture. It was first published in the spring of 1932, and a few months later Wright and his wife Olgivanna announced that they planned to accept apprentices-in-residence, beginning in October. They called the program the "Taliesin Fellowship." Robert F. Bishop, who meant to visit Taliesin only for a short time, in the summer of 1932, and then stayed nearly three years, not long ago described the Fellowship as a studio-workshop situation "somewhat akin to the studio-work-

shops of the Renaissance, but with a collective farm thrown in."[2] Originally there were about 40 apprentices and assistants, and whether or not they paid their "tuition" they gained no academic credit whatsoever. They did learn, soon enough, that they were obliged to perform tasks which seemed to have little to do with their training as architects: besides sawing oak, quarrying sandstone and operating a lime kiln to furnish the materials for remodelings and extensions of the Taliesin buildings, they grew vegetables, cooked, served, washed dishes and cleaned house. "Outside of the Studio," Edgar Tafel has recalled of the winters of 1932 and 1933, "we kept in trim by going off to the woods every other day to fell trees as fuel for the boilers and fireplaces. Half of the Fellowship was keeping the other half warm."[3] Such experiences were not forgotten; despite the menial labor, few of the apprentices seem to have regretted their years with Wright.

Wright's *Autobiography* affected many people in many ways. In 1934, when Edgar Kaufmann, jr., was 24 years old and back from a long stay in Europe, a friend of his in New York (a woman who worked as a secretary in an art gallery) spoke to him about the book with great enthusiasm. He soon read it with a deep sense of personal discovery; nearly 30 years later he could recall that "I had no inkling of the character of his art, and his story flowed into my mind like the first trickle of irrigation in a desert land."[4] After talking to his parents about Wright, Edgar Kaufmann, jr., went to Taliesin for an interview, on September 27, as a candidate for apprenticeship. It

---

[1] Wright, "In the Cause of Architecture—The Terms," *Architectural Record*, 64 (Dec. 1928), p. 512.

[2] Robert F. Bishop, Southampton, Pa. Letter of June 21, 1974. Wright had always attracted young assistants, but without any formal system.

[3] *Prairie School Review*, V (4th quarter, 1968), p. 27.

[4] "Twenty-five Years of the House on the Waterfall," *L'architettura—cronache e storia*, 82 (Aug. 1962), p. 39. From 1924 to 1927, Edgar Kaufmann, jr., attended the Shady Side Academy, in Pittsburgh, which his father also had attended. In the following years he studied painting in New York, at the Kunstgewerbeschule in Vienna and with Victor Hammer in Florence and London. He returned to America in mid-1934.

was only six days later that Wright asked his secretary, Eugene Masselink, to mail to E. J. Kaufmann a copy of *The Life-Work of the American Architect Frank Lloyd Wright*, a sumptuous book published in Holland in 1925. Wright was never slow to sense a prospective client. Kaufmann had no special awareness of Wright, his son has recalled, other than remotely: Benno Janssen, a Pittsburgh architect who with his partner W. Y. Cocken had designed for the Kaufmanns a house built in 1924–1925 in the Fox Chapel borough, and had redesigned the main floor of Kaufmann's Store in an Art Moderne style (it was opened again in May 1930), knew such prominent stage and industrial designers as Norman Bel Geddes, Joseph Urban and Paul T. Frankl—all of whom knew Wright.[5]

Although he had no plans for a career in architecture, Edgar Kaufmann, jr., joined the Taliesin Fellowship on October 15, 1934. Wright had heard in the meantime about plans for an exposition in New York where he might be able to exhibit; it was an opportunity to revive his project for a prototype American community. His book called *The Disappearing City*, published in the fall of 1932, had met with little success, and hardly without reason—the text was as vague as it was brief, and the illustrations (there were only six) gave no idea of what he had in mind for the ideal city. "Broadacre City," as he had named it, cried out for expression in plans and models.

E. J. Kaufmann, who later became a founding member of the Allegheny Conference on Community Development, wrote Wright on October 20 about some possible civic projects in Pittsburgh, and Wright answered that he would, indeed, be interested in helping the city. Kaufmann and his wife were planning a trip to Taliesin to visit their son and to meet Wright and his wife. They arrived on November 16.

Kaufmann at 49 years old was an exceptionally successful businessman who loved to build things, and he was by all accounts just as his son has described him, "a magnetic and unconventional person." He possessed every quality that Wright admired in a client. (Nearly a

year later, when Kaufmann was obliged to introduce Wright as a speaker to The Hungry Club, in Pittsburgh, he would say that "although Mr. Wright has always faced the severest opposition from officialdom—public and professional—there has rarely been a moment during his long career when he has not found an appreciative client among a group of open-minded, sincere American business men and women who realized from their own experience the value, or at least part of it, of what he had to give them in spite of the lack of seals and red tape around his reputation." John H. Howe, one of Wright's chief lieutenants, recalled recently that "Mr. Wright and Mr. Kaufmann had great rapport from the start, each with genuine admiration for the other.")[6]

Wright and Kaufmann talked about Pittsburgh, and particularly a proposal for a planetarium there.[7] They also talked about Broadacre City; for the New York exposition Wright was eager to complete a large model, 12 feet square. It was not long after the Kaufmanns had visited him that Wright asked for help. He wired Kaufmann on December 3 that he needed 500 dollars. Kaufmann sent him the money promptly, and later sent another 500 dollars. But by December 7 Wright had written that a floor plan of the exposition, which had come, showed the space allotted Wright to be so small that the model would be rendered insignificant. So, farewell to Broadacre City from New York, said Wright; but Kaufmann of course was welcome to show it in his store. In mid-December, Wright met Kaufmann in Pittsburgh to discuss the planetarium project and also the possibility of designing for Kaufmann a new office on the top floor of the store building. Then they went down to Bear Run.

Kaufmann and his wife had been thinking about a new weekend house, and their son had suggested that Wright might well design it. Their problem came from the road that passed through Mill Run and Ohiopyle (now Penn-

[5] Benno Janssen (1874–1964) was adept at various styles. His picturesquely medieval brick house for the Kaufmanns is illustrated in James D. Van Trump and Arthur P. Ziegler, jr., *Landmark Architecture of Allegheny County Pennsylvania* (Pittsburgh, 1967), p. 191. Norman Bel Geddes (1893–1958) met Wright in 1916 through Aline Barnsdall, for whom Wright was planning a house and theater. Geddes liked neither design, and he also told Wright, when they were touring Oak Park, Ill., that his Unity Temple looked like a library. Joseph Urban (1872–1933) had designed a swimming pool for the Irene Kaufmann Settlement House in Pittsburgh, an institution founded by Edgar J. Kaufmann's uncle, Henry Kaufmann. Paul T. Frankl (1886–1958)—a Viennese, as was Urban—dedicated his book *New Dimensions* (New York, 1928) to Wright.

[6] John H. Howe, Minneapolis. Letter of Dec. 31, 1973. In *An Autobiography* (all citations will be from the revised edition, New York, 1943), p. 448, Wright described Kaufmann as "a good business man as well as a good fellow too." Wright expressed his appreciation for American businessmen as clients in his "In the Cause of Architecture—Second Paper," *Architectural Record*, 34 (May 1914), p. 409, and in his introduction to *Ausgeführte Bauten und Entwürfe von Frank Lloyd Wright* (Berlin, 1910). In a symposium held at Columbia University in May 1964, the historian Sibyl Moholy-Nagy remarked that "when you think of the fact that Mr. Wright was able in 1908 to persuade a bicycle manufacturer in Chicago [F. C. Robie] to finance a plan of such absolutely scandalous novelty [for a house at Fifty-eighth and Woodlawn], this is for me infinitely greater than almost anything that was later done in Europe."

[7] At the May 1964 symposium at Columbia University, Edgar Kaufmann, jr., observed that by the mid-1920s a planetarium had become "the newest symbol of the popular appeal of science." Wright in 1925 designed a planetarium housed within a ziggurat-like automobile lookout, for a site northwest of Washington, D.C. The plans came to nothing.

sylvania Route 381), which was paved in 1930; although Kaufmann had been a booster of the project, the road passed below the cliff where the cabin stood, and each year there seemed to be more traffic, noise and fumes, particularly on Saturday nights. The little Aladdin cabin hardly served as a country retreat. What the Kaufmanns wanted was a year-round weekend house, a house with the modern conveniences, away from the highway, deeper in the forest, and closer to the waterfalls, where they most liked to go for sunning, bathing and picnicking. The house should have (besides a living and dining space) a master bedroom, a separate dressing room, a bedroom for Edgar Kaufmann, jr., a guest bedroom and, eventually, a wing for the servants and for more guest accommodations.

Wright looked at the stream, the falls, the trees, the rock ledges and the boulders. He had written a few years earlier something about what rock meant to him:

> The rock-ledges of a stone-quarry are a story and a longing to me. There is suggestion in the strata and character in the formations. I like to sit and feel it, as it is. Often I have thought, were great monumental buildings ever given me to build, I would go to the Grand Canyon of Arizona to ponder them . . . . For in the stony bone-work of the Earth, the principles that shaped stone as it lies, or as it rises and remains to be sculptured by winds and tide—there sleep forms and styles enough for all the ages for all of Man.[8]

Wright told Kaufmann he would need a contour map, one which would also show the position of every boulder and every large tree. After he had returned to Taliesin he wrote Kaufmann on December 26, 1934, how the visit to the waterfalls remained with him, and how a house had taken vague shape in his mind to the music of the stream.

Wright already had made plans to move the Fellowship to Arizona for the winter; he was getting older and colder at his home in Wisconsin, and to heat the buildings there either cost 3500 dollars or took half the time of the apprentices.[9] He told Kaufmann that the Fellowship would camp at Chandler, on a mesa east of Phoenix; Kaufmann wrote that he and his wife would like to make reservations at Chandler too.[10] The apprentices drove to Arizona in January and resumed work on Broadacre City—the models would be shown in New York after all, because more space was being reserved for Wright's exhibit.

[8] Wright, "The Meaning of Materials—Stone," *Architectural Record*, 63 (April 1928), pp. 350, 356.
[9] Wright, *An Autobiography*, p. 452. In October 1935, Wright wrote Kaufmann about buying coal wholesale in Pennsylvania.
[10] Chandler was founded by Dr. Alexander Chandler, who commissioned one of Wright's most beautiful (but unexecuted) projects of the 1920s, the vast winter resort "San Marcos-in-the-Desert."

Mr. and Mrs. Kaufmann left Pittsburgh for Arizona on February 14. For some reason—severe weather, perhaps—a topographic map of the Bear Run site had not been made. Wright must have told the Kaufmanns that he could not proceed without the map; a memorandum of February 20 in the files of Morris Knowles, Engineers, notes the need to furnish a "plane table survey" very quickly: "Mr. Kaufmann wishes particularly to identify the larger trees and the character of the rock outcrops. . . . Mr. Kaufmann is particularly anxious to have the survey cleaned up this week as he is thinking of building a house at the camp in the spring."

The map was finished March 9 [11]. It showed every tree of at least six inches in diameter, and it noted that the boulders and rock outcrops were of hard sandstone. Only a small area was surveyed (the scale was one inch to 20 feet), and the wooden truss bridge a short way east of the falls was at the upper right-hand corner of the map; the rest of the map reached westward past the falls. From the area surveyed, it could be surmised that Kaufmann expected the house to be downstream from the

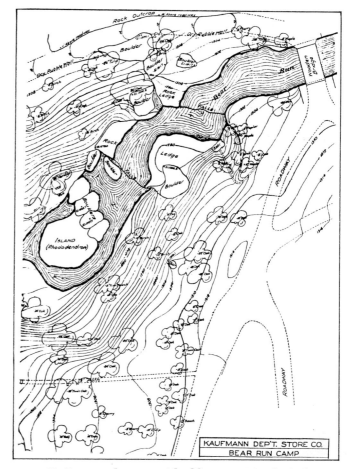

11. *Topographic map of building site, March 1935.*

falls, and that whatever Wright had vaguely in mind he was keeping to himself.

By now, Kaufmann was more than a client of Wright's: he was a patron. Except for the plans of a house for Stanley Marcus, and for one or two much smaller houses of the kind Wright was to call "Usonian," every prospect that the Fellowship saw for 1935 was connected with Kaufmann—the weekend house, the office interior, the planetarium project and various models of Broadacre City.[11]

The models came first. They were due to go on exhibition in New York on April 15. "The trip was *literally* 'en charrette,' the meaning of which you will appreciate if you know the Parisian Beaux-Arts origin of the term," Robert F. Bishop recently recalled, referring to students who had to compete against strict deadlines and thus hastened to get their projects on the passing charrette, a cart for collecting the drawings. "We started late, allowed just enough time to make the grand opening, then ran into and through the worst dust-storm on record, clear across the lengthy state of Kansas. Though dusty and forlorn, we made it." Bishop was traveling with Edgar Tafel, Edgar Kaufmann, jr., and Byron Keeler (Bob) Mosher. They took turns driving a small car which belonged to Kaufmann and a truck which carried the models and announced itself as Wright's emissary by its color, red, and by its Taliesin insigne, a tight linear pattern within a square. To Wright the square "potently" suggested integrity. Red was his favorite color and was likewise symbolic. "The color red is invincible," he quoted Timiriazev, the plant physiologist, as saying. "It is the color not only of the blood—it is the color of creation. It is the only life-giving color in nature filling the sprouting plant with life and giving warmth to everything in creation. . . ."[12]

The models were taken to the Industrial Arts Exposition in the Forum of Rockefeller Center, and installed under Wright's banner proclaiming "A New Freedom." Wright himself arrived in time for the opening; he was to be one of the speakers. ("As everyone knows, we live in economic, aesthetic and moral chaos," he said, "for the reason that American life has achieved no organic form."

An architect, he emphasized, "should at least see life as organic form continually.")

"Bob Mosher and I manned the show," Tafel remembers, "and Mr. Wright was staying at the Lafayette Hotel. We all took a trip to Southampton with a possible client. Actually, Mr. Wright was trying to look for publicity and new clients through the exhibition."[13] So far as publicity, he did well; his speech was reported in the *Times*, and Broadacre City got good notice in *The New Yorker* and in both the *Architectural Record* and the *American Architect*.[14] In New York, the notion of a planned community based on a minimum of one acre for the childless couple, more space for the larger family and a motor car for every citizen must have seemed pure fantasy. Wright nevertheless quite accurately presented the models as an interpretation of the tendencies in American growth. (By 1970, the census found more persons living in suburbs than in cities.) So central to Broadacre City was the motor car that some of the collateral models illustrating types of dwellings were identified by the numbers of cars they harbored. One, designated as the "two-car" residence, had certain features which would appear more forcefully in the house on Bear Run: a broad cantilevered terrace and a flat roof slab perforated to form a horizontal trellis.

Wright wrote Kaufmann on April 27 that he was ready to go to work on plans for the planetarium and for the weekend house. He evidently saw Kaufmann again in May; a memorandum in Wright's hand indicates that he was in Pittsburgh on May 18. Kaufmann wrote to him on May 22 that he would be interested in having sketches made for the house and for the office (he had mailed a blueprint of the floor plan to Wright on December 21), but first he wanted an estimate on how much the sketches might cost.

In Pittsburgh, the models of Broadacre City became part of "New Homes for Old," an exposition sponsored by the Federal Housing Administration. It opened on June

[11] The house for Marcus was never built. Mr. and Mrs. Paul Hanna discussed a house with Wright in June 1935, before they had a site; their "Honeycomb" house in Palo Alto, Calif., was not built until 1937.
[12] *Architectural Forum*, 68 (Jan. 1938), foll. p. 102. Kliment Arkadevich Timiriazev (1843–1920) was best known in this country as the author of *The Life of the Plant*, already in its seventh revised edition by 1912. Wright's interest in such studies paralleled Louis H. Sullivan's attention to such writers as Asa Gray. Wright's little insigne somehow managed to be different from any of the 3064 designs collected and published by Flinders Petrie in *Decorative Patterns of the Ancient World* (London, 1930; Dover reprint, 1974), though Petrie no doubt would have classified it under the "complex key patterns" (cf. his plate LXXVII).

[13] Edgar Tafel, New York. Letter of July 29, 1974. Bishop and Edgar Kaufmann, jr., left the Fellowship after the trip to New York.
[14] *New York Times*, April 16, 1935, p. 23; Lewis Mumford, "The Sky Line," *The New Yorker*, 11 (April 27, 1935), pp. 79–80; *Architectural Record*, 77 (April 1935), pp. 243–254; *American Architect*, 146 (May 1935), pp. 55–62. Mumford was much impressed: "Broadacre City . . . is both a generous dream and a rational plan . . . . On the whole, Wright's philosophy of life and his mode of planning have never shown to better advantage." Many years later, however, he noted that the plan "made every social activity call for long distance transportation and therefore the incessant use of the motor car," and he called it merely a coherent pattern for the random forces that have disintegrated the American city; see *Architectural Record*, 132 (Dec. 1962), p. 102. In *A Testament* (New York, 1957), p. 179, Wright still held hope for decentralization and "organic reintegration," but he acknowledged that "Both the life of town and country now waste each other. Accelerated by the exaggerated motor car . . . ."

18, on the eleventh floor of Kaufmann's Store. A few of the apprentices were on hand for the opening, but Wright was not; he introduced himself by writing for the *Sun-Telegraph*. "The principle Allegheny County seems to have put to work is 'to hell with nature, and we'll get what we want in spite of her,'" he wrote, offending an editorialist, who hastened to label Wright a "dreamer," and also William N. McNair, the mayor, who soon objected that Broadacre City was only a utopian scheme, and one both paternalistic and socialistic. Wright's ideas about city planning were a natural extension of his ideas about individual dwellings, or dwellings for individuals, and while writing about Pittsburgh he was evidently thinking about Bear Run:

> Well—at this late day it isn't good medicine, perhaps, to imagine (now) how the river might have been made into a beautiful feature by damming and pooling it into placid water and driving across the broad dams to the tune of waterfalls, into and up to broad terraced levels picturesquely related to the water . . . .[15]

When he arrived in Pittsburgh and was taken on a tour of the city, on June 29 (it was the last day of the exposition, and also of the store's sixty-fourth anniversary sale), Wright made sarcastic remarks about everything but the Court House and County Jail, both of which he recognized as by H. H. Richardson, one of the few architects in his youth for whom, later, he professed any respect at all. The tour was planned to end with the model residential area of Chatham Village, where the Buhl Foundation had just announced plans for 68 more brick row houses. "It's a great way to sell bricks," Wright was reported to have said. Finally, when someone asked him how he would rebuild Pittsburgh, he answered: "It would be cheaper to abandon it . . . ."[16]

One of the Taliesin apprentices, Blaine Drake, recalls driving Wright to Bear Run sometime in the summer of 1935. Drake writes that he was not aware, at the time, that Wright already had seen the site:

> He never mentioned that to me on our drive to Bear Run from Taliesin and it was his nature to talk freely most of the time when we were driving. Perhaps his

having been there explains why he was able to describe so completely his concept of the ultimate design, as he usually wasn't in a hurry to begin a new design . . . . The finished design was as I visualized it when he was talking to the Kaufmanns. I remember E. J. being quite surprised that the house would be above the falls. He told F. Ll. W. he had always expected the house to be on the opposite side of the Run, looking at the falls from below . . . .[17]

Kaufmann wrote Wright on July 5 that he hoped his new office could be constructed that summer and be ready for use in September. He also said the house on Bear Run should be planned so as to cost between 20,000 and 30,000 dollars. Wright began the sketches for the office first; on August 21 he promised Kaufmann some results soon. The next day Kaufmann sent him a retainer of 250 dollars for sketches of the house. He may have been anxious; certainly the apprentices were. Wright did not like to rush to the drawing board, as Drake remembers. John Lautner, another apprentice, puts it this way: "He had the design totally in his head, as always, and as he recommended to the apprentices, if no whole idea, no architecture."[18] Wright once wrote:

> . . . conceive the building in the imagination, not on paper but in the mind, thoroughly—before touching paper. Let it live there—gradually taking more definite form before committing it to the draughting board. When the thing lives for you—start to plan it with tools. Not before . . . Working on it with triangle and T square should modify or extend or intensify or test the conception—complete the harmonious adjustment of its parts.[19]

Few of Wright's associates remember that he waited so long to put his ideas down on paper. He probably would have waited even longer if he had not heard, by August 26, that Kaufmann and Irwin D. Wolf, vice-president of the store, intended to be in Milwaukee for a meeting of the Cavendish consortium of retailers, and were planning to drive to Taliesin afterward, on September 22. Kaufmann was eager to see the plans for his new house. He did not ask if there were any.

About that Sunday when Wright made his first sketches of Fallingwater there are various and conflicting accounts: in 40 years memory can play strange tricks.

[15] Wright, "Broadacres to Pittsburgh," *Pittsburgh Sun-Telegraph*, June 24, 1935, ed. page. Reports on the exposition appeared in the same paper on June 14, p. 12, and June 18, p. 8. Wright published a revised version of his article in *Taliesin*, 1 (Oct. 1940), pp. 30–32, as well as his speech at the exposition in New York (pp. 35–37).

[16] See James A. Baubie, "Flings Sneers at Pittsburgh," *Sun-Telegraph*, June 30, 1935, part I, p. 13. Chatham Village is often rated one of the most successfully designed housing projects in the nation; e.g., see Norman T. Newton, *Design on the Land* (Cambridge, Mass., 1971), pp. 496–500. Pittsburgh has never been allowed to forget Wright's final comment about abandoning it: see *Time*, July 15, 1935, p. 44; *Life*, Aug. 12, 1946, p. 94; *Landscape Architecture*, April 1963, p. 209; *National Geographic*, March 1965, p. 343; and *TWA Ambassador*, May 1974, pp. 31, 35.

[17] Blaine Drake, Phoenix, Ariz. Letter of May 19, 1975. Drake joined the Fellowship in January 1933 and stayed until the summer of 1941. Other apprentices recall Kaufmann having no idea of the house until being shown the first sketches. Prof. J. F. Kienitz, who evidently had access to Taliesin, in "The Romanticism of Frank Lloyd Wright," *Art in America*, 32 (April 1944), pp. 99–101, wrote that Wright saw Bear Run only once before Kaufmann's visit to Taliesin forced him to make the first sketches.

[18] John Lautner, Los Angeles. Letter of June 20, 1974. Lautner was an apprentice from 1933 to 1939.

[19] Wright, "In the Cause of Architecture: The Logic of the Plan," *Architectural Record*, 63 (Jan. 1928), p. 49.

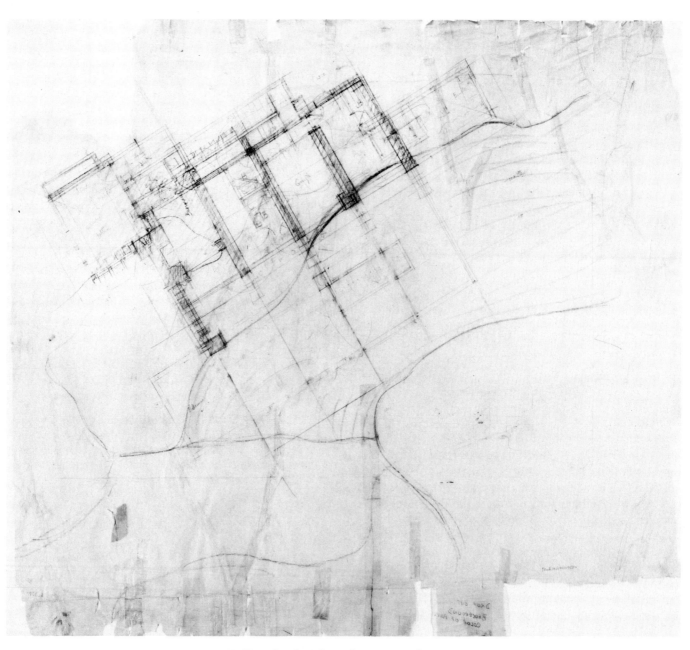

12. First sketch of floor plans, September 1935.

John Lautner recalls Wright working from the topographic map and getting his ideas down on tracing paper within 15 or 20 minutes. Blaine Drake thinks Wright began the sketches immediately after they returned from Bear Run, and chose to work in private. "He usually enjoyed an audience while he was working . . . . This was his way of teaching," Drake writes. "But this day he said, 'Boys, I would like to work on this alone.'" Cornelia Brierly, another apprentice, who had been in Pittsburgh with the Broadacre City models, recalled not long ago that Wright made his sketches so early one morning that the apprentices were surprised to see them already on his drafting table as they passed through the studio on their way to breakfast, at 6:30.

Bob Mosher and Edgar Tafel, who had met Kaufmann while traveling with the models, were the apprentices who became most intimately involved with the house on Bear Run. Mosher likes to recall Wright beginning to work only after getting a telephone call from Kaufmann, who was just leaving Milwaukee for Taliesin. Mosher continues:

Mr. Wright was not at all disturbed by the fact that not one line had been drawn. As was normal, he asked me to bring him the topographical map of Bear Run, to his draughting table in the sloping-roofed studio at Taliesin, a rustic but wondrous room in itself . . . . I stood by, on his right side, keeping his colored-pencils sharpened. Every line he drew, vertically and especially horizontally, I watched with complete fascination . . . . Mr. Kaufmann arrived and Mr. Wright greeted him in his wondrously warm manner. In the studio, Mr. Wright explained the sketches to his client. Mr. Kaufmann, a very intelligent but practical gentleman, merely said . . . "I thought you would place the house near the waterfall, not over it." Mr. Wright said quietly, "E. J., I want you to live with the waterfall, not just to look at it, but for it to become an integral part of your lives." And it did just that. That evening, my colleague Edgar Tafel and I stayed up very late and drew pencil perspectives looking up and looking down. Early the next morning, Mr. Wright came into the studio, took my perspective, and finished it with his inevitable colored-pencils.[20]

Edgar Tafel recalls that before Kaufmann arrived that morning Wright had sketched all the floor plans (on top of each other [12], and in different colors for different floors), a north-south section through the house, and a south elevation, or straight-on view, of the side that came as close as any to being the front [13]. So far as Kaufmann knew, the sketches had been ready for some time. Wright explained them, then led Kaufmann away to lunch; Tafel and Mosher lingered behind and missed

their meal in order to dash off two more elevation sketches. Wright returned with Kaufmann, and rather casually took up the sketches, saying, "And, E. J., here's the west elevation . . . and here's the north elevation."[21]

Wright had kept the idea in his mind for exactly nine months. His sketches may have looked a little rough to Kaufmann, but they turned out to be a remarkably complete presentation of the house as it would be built: the house had been conceived with an awesome finality [14, 15]. Behind the pencils in his hand stood an imagination as disciplined as it was free. He was well into the fourth decade of his mature practice, and he was able to realize as much as his imagination could suggest. "You see," he once wrote, "by way of concentrated thought, the idea is likely to spring into life all at once and be completed eventually with the unity of a living organism."[22]

When he was asked about the house many years later, Wright made it sound almost easy:

There in a beautiful forest was a solid, high rock ledge rising beside a waterfall, and the natural thing seemed to be to cantilever the house from that rock bank over the falling water . . . . Then came (of course) Mr. Kaufmann's love for the beautiful site. He loved the site where the house was built and liked to listen to the waterfall. So that was a prime motive in the design. I

[20] Byron Keeler Mosher, Marbella, Spain. Letter of Jan. 20, 1974. Mosher recalled his later experiences at Bear Run in conversations between May 15 and May 17, 1974, at his home.

[21] Edgar Tafel, in a conversation of June 12, 1974.
[22] Wright, in the *Architectural Forum*, 94 (Jan. 1951), p. 93.

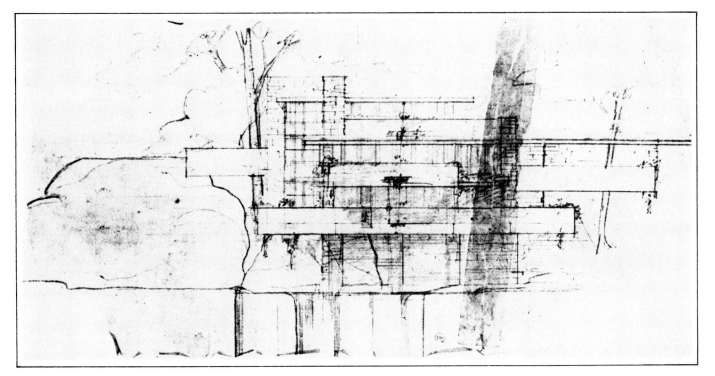

13. First sketch of south elevation, September 1935.

think you can hear the waterfall when you look at the design. At least it is there, and he lives intimately with the thing he loves.[23]

On his first visit to Bear Run, Wright must have noticed the old bridge across the stream, the roadway turning against the high and solid ledge, and the Porter cottage high on the hill [see 10], all of which already suggested a site on the north side of the stream. And he had his own rule about orientation: any house not confined by the usual narrow city lot, he said, should be addressed "30–60" to the south, so that every room could be cheered by sunlight for at least part of the day.

A house on the south side of the stream, where Kaufmann seemed to have imagined it, could hardly be so oriented unless, perversely enough, it turned its back to the most distinctive feature of the site. To put the house as near as possible to the upper waterfall, to tuck it between the stream and the rock cliff, and to give it the best orientation, Wright aligned it parallel to the old bridge. This he accomplished in his first sketch, drawn on top of the contour map; with north at the top, his T square set the east-west line, and he used it only to support his 30–60 triangle (the 30-degree angle at the left, the 60-degree angle at the upper right). The south front of the house thus could be drawn along the hypotenuse, establishing the axis of orientation at 30 degrees east of due south (or seven and one-half degrees east of south-south-east). By simply turning his triangle on end, Wright had the guide for every line perpendicular to the south front of the house.

The house on Bear Run was to serve the Kaufmanns on their weekends away from an active business life in the city. It was to be a country house, in communion with the forest and the stream. Wright conceived the house in terms of living space extended into the forest and above the falls, on terraces echoing the ledges of rock beneath the stream and along the cliffs: to him the rock ledges suggested terraces projected into space [16, 17]. He had spent the summers of his adolescent years in the Wyoming Valley of Wisconsin, where the sandstone cropped out in thin ledges; when he built Taliesin there, some 25 years before he began to think about the house on Bear Run, he had the walls laid up in courses of sandstone—rough, random, shifting ledges.[24] Now he could imagine

an entire house constituted from a series of terraces, staggered but secure, like the ancient rock ledges. He described the house as essentially an "extension of the cliff beside a mountain stream, making living space over and above the stream upon several terraces upon which a man who loved the place sincerely, one who liked to listen to the waterfall, might well live."[25]

How could such terraces of space—a house, as he phrased it, seemingly "leaping out from the rock ledge behind"—be built without direct vertical supports, which would intrude on the natural beauty of the stream? By means of the cantilever, a beam system extended beyond its support. Wright saw the cantilever as a profoundly natural principle, as in the outstretched arm, or the tree branch growing from the trunk. He thought that engineers had failed to grasp its real potentialities; that, with imagination, it could become the most romantic and most free of all principles of construction. The cantilever, he said, could perform remarkable things in liberating space and creating planes parallel to the earth, those long and continuous horizontal planes and lines that he believed to be the essential expression "of human tenure on this earth," "the true earth-line of human life, indicative of freedom. Always."[26]

The house would have a "definite masonry form" to be in sympathy with its site. But of course the cantilevers, on such scale, could not be of stone. For the first time in his experience, Wright said, reinforced concrete was truly necessary in building a residence. In itself, concrete was not a material that Wright found of interest. It was passive and without intrinsic aesthetic character. But it could be cast into any form; it was completely plastic; and it had the exceptional property of growing ever stronger with age. When it was reinforced with steel, concrete acquired extraordinary tensile strength.

[25] Wright, in the *Architectural Forum*, 68 (Jan. 1938), p. 36.
[26] Wright, *A Testament*, p. 219, and *An Autobiography*, p. 349. Although an ancient principle, the cantilever appeared traditionally in small-scale details such as balconies or stairs. Even then, it was associated with special moments in architectural space. Nineteenth-century bridge engineering vastly enlarged the role of the cantilever. Skyscraper engineering soon adopted the cantilever, too; in his earliest days as an architect in Chicago, Wright could see commercial space being created above the sidewalks in projecting "oriel" bays. By 1889–1890 the side walls of such buildings were being carried on huge girders cantilevered beyond the line of foundation piers. Wright often used the cantilever in his early prairie houses, but hardly with such daring as on Bear Run. He seated most of the congregation of the Unity Temple (1905–1909) in balconies. He used cantilever construction throughout the Imperial Hotel in Tokyo, but specifically to resist earthquake damage. Various of his unexecuted projects of the 1920s—a skyscraper in Chicago, the St. Mark's Apartments in New York and the Elizabeth Noble Apartments in Los Angeles—relied on the cantilever principle. Edgar Kaufmann, jr., points out that a direct ancestor of the concrete cantilevers at Bear Run can be found in François Hennebique's house at Bourg-la-Reine, south of Paris, begun in 1904; see the section drawing in Sigfried Giedion, *Space, Time and Architecture,* 4th ed. (Cambridge, Mass., 1963), p. 322.

[23] Wright, in an interview at Taliesin with Hugh Downs, © 1953 by the National Broadcasting Company.
[24] In his conversation with Hugh Downs, Wright spoke of the wooded site and protruding rock ledges in Wisconsin and commented that "the same thought applied to Taliesin that applied later to Bear Run. The site determined the features and character of Taliesin." He may have begun Taliesin as early as 1909. Something of its character is forecast in his 1908 project for a lodge at Estes Park, Colo., where, interestingly enough, one bedroom wing would have spanned a mountain stream. See *Ausgeführte Bauten und Entwürfe von Frank Lloyd Wright* (Berlin, 1910), plate 38.

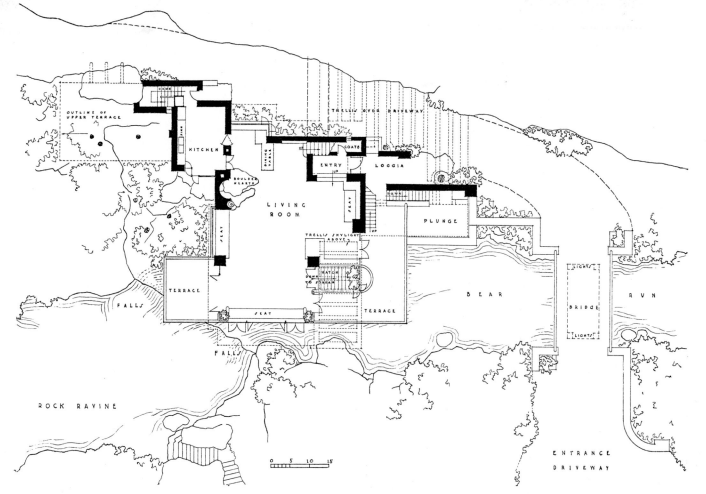

ABOVE: *14. Plan of first floor.* BELOW: *15. Plans of second and third floors, and elevations.*

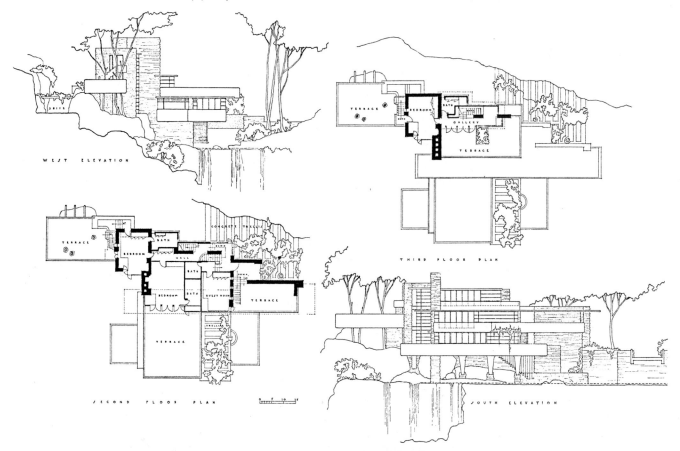

ABOVE LEFT: *16. Rock ledges along Bear Run.* ABOVE RIGHT: *17. Stone masonry of bridge terminal, Fallingwater.* LEFT: *18. Quarrying stones for the house, 1936.* OPPOSITE: *19. Perspective study of Fallingwater by Wright.*

By the waterfalls on Bear Run, where the land was so ragged and precipitous, and the horizon line scarcely visible, an overriding rhythm of horizontal planes and lines became all the more essential to give the living space of the house the expansive and adventurous freedom that Wright believed to be basic to American life [see 23]. The house would welcome the changes of season, of weather, of the light of day; at the same time, in those darker and more secure spaces shaped by the great masses of stone masonry that counterbalanced the cantilevered terraces, there would be comforting warmth and a sense of shelter and refuge, where the steady sound from the falls would reinforce the forest quiet.

Wright had waited for the whole idea, and now he had it. "I hope you will continue to work on the house plan," Kaufmann wrote him on September 27, "so that we can get our preliminary sketches, floor plans and elevations at the very earliest possible time. . . ." His son wrote Wright the same day: "Father spent quite some time at Bear Run showing just where the various rooms would be and Edgar [Tafel] sent a rough drawing of the wall masses so that we are all tremendously anxious to see just what the house really will look like."

The preliminary plans for both the house and the office were mailed from Taliesin on October 15. Wright had left the day before, to lecture at Yale; on the 19th he arrived in Pittsburgh for another lecture. He met Kaufmann and visited Bear Run again. A month later he wrote Kaufmann that they should assume the minimum cost of the house and furnishings would run 35,000 dollars.

Near the end of the year an old quarry was opened on the hill about 500 feet west of the falls. Kaufmann wrote Wright on December 12 that about five cords of stone were being taken each week. "They are taking the strata of the stone as it comes and breaking it up in pieces about 12″ to 14″ wide and 24″ long, the thickness being the strata of the quarry," he said [18]. A few months before his death in 1976, the contractor, Norbert James (N. J.) Zeller, recalled how his men had chopped lines four feet back from the edge of the rock, then set off rows of dynamite caps to break it loose. The stones were carried down from the hill on a horse-drawn sled.

Wright was still at work on the drawings, and John H. Howe remembers that winter very well:

It would be hard to convey the excitement that we at Taliesin felt when Mr. Kaufmann asked Mr. Wright to design his house for Bear Run. This followed many years of unexecuted projects in the Taliesin studio, and together with the Johnson Wax commission indicated that the coming years would be ones of great fulfillment for Taliesin . . . . I particularly remember Mr. Wright as he worked with relish early one morning on the perspective drawings of Fallingwater; he was dressed in his bathrobe, seated at a table by the fire in his study-bedroom. I had brought the layouts in from the studio, and was standing by with a supply of colored pencils, while he worked on the drawings. The most satisfactory and beautifully executed of these drawings [19] was later published on the cover of the January 17, 1938, issue of *Time* magazine, as background to Mr. Wright's portrait . . . . This drawing is one which was executed entirely by Mr. Wright himself.[27]

27 John H. Howe, letter of Dec. 31, 1973. The commission for the Johnson Administration Building in Racine, Wis., was first discussed in the summer of 1936; see *An Autobiography*, pp. 468–469. According to E. Willis Jones, Wright initially attempted to convince executives of the Johnson company to build an entirely new factory and company-town west of Racine—apparently, a bid to implement ideas from the Broadacre City studies. See *The Inland Architect*, 13 (Aug.-Sept. 1969), p. 18.

Chapter III
CONSTRUCTION BEGINS: 1936

Very few changes were made when the more detailed drawings for Fallingwater were finished in January 1936. One of them was Wright's decision to round the horizontal edges of the parapets and roof slabs as a more just expression of the nature of the material, reinforced concrete. Another was his rounding, in plan, of the parapet itself where it swung around the east end of the stairwell leading from the living room down to the stream [20]. With both these changes he introduced the semicircle as a secondary motif in his design, and once it was introduced, he played it throughout the house. "The sound constitution of any entity," he wrote, "is pregnant with graceful reflexes."[1]

Bob Mosher and Edgar Tafel worked on most of the detailed drawings. Blaine Drake remembers working on some, and a few months later, when structural calculations had to be made, Mendel Glickman and William Wesley Peters were also involved [21]. Two sets of blueprints and three sets of specifications were sent to Kaufmann on February 24. He was in Europe in March; on April 3 he wrote Wright to say that he had returned and studied the plans with no end of thrills. "We are constructing a sample wall," he added. But he had already sent the drawings to his consulting engineers, Morris Knowles.

Abrom Dombar, who had been an apprentice at Taliesin, was working at Kaufmann's Store as the assistant display architect; he had been a friend of Edgar Kaufmann, jr., at Taliesin, and now they often went to Bear Run on weekends. Dombar remembers the Kaufmanns studying the plans for the new house. "The plans were given to the Pittsburgh engineers to determine whether the site was capable of supporting the concentrated load of the building," he recalls.[2] The engineers were not convinced by Wright's drawings or by his idea of building a house above a waterfall. They sent their report to Kaufmann on April 3:

In accordance with your request, we have reviewed the plans prepared by Mr. Wright for your house at Bear Run, and offer the following comments . . . .

1. The end of one of the foundation walls is shown to be approximately 15 feet from the crest of the waterfall. There is a possibility of future undercutting sufficient to endanger the foundation at this point. We do not know the rate at which the falls are receding . . . .

2. At the time of flood the foundation walls will deflect the main current in the stream toward the east bank at the crest of the waterfall. This may result in erosion of earth from the rock surface and tend to shift the falls to the eastward . . . [we] call your attention to the possibility of some alteration in the appearance of the falls.

3. The stone foundation walls which project into the stream—the upper one particularly—should be strong enough to withstand the battering of heavy driftwood at time of flood. We suggest that they be keyed into the rock ledge and be constructed three feet, instead of two feet, in thickness . . . .

4. We have no information concerning probable stability of the large boulder to be incorporated into the structure . . . and we question seriously the advisability of utilizing it as a part of the building foundation.

5. The plans . . . do not show dimensions of principal supporting members of the building, nor structural details such as arrangement of steel reinforcement . . . . Without this information, it is of course impossible to check the structural design of the building for strength and safety . . . .

6. . . . The plans do not show sufficient information to check the strength and stability of the proposed bridge.

7. . . . there is always a possibility of an extreme flood, and this might bring water as high as the boiler room floor.

8. . . . approval of the state Water and Power Resources Board is required for construction or alteration of bridges, walls and other possible obstructions to stream flow . . . .[3]

---

[1] Wright, *An Autobiography*, p. 309. Henry-Russell Hitchcock has written that "reflex" was a favorite word of Wright's, and certainly the concept is basic to Wright's ideal of consistent character in the building as a work of art.

[2] Abrom Dombar, Cincinnati, Ohio. Letter of April 4, 1975. Dombar joined the Fellowship in October 1932 and left it three years later, "when the creditors were pounding at Taliesin's doors."

[3] Copies of this report and others in the long succession of engineers' inspections of the house are in the Avery Library.

20. East living-room terrace and curved parapet at stairwell.

"Mr. Kaufmann sent the report to Mr. Wright," Dombar recalls. "Mr. Wright told Mr. K. to send the drawings back to Taliesin ('since he did not deserve the house'), whereupon Mr. K. apologized and said to go ahead with the working-drawings."

There were in fact two reports. The engineers returned to Bear Run on April 16 because Kaufmann asked them to check again for erosion at the falls, to study more closely the boulder that Wright intended to use as the anchor of the house, and to stake out the foundation lines so that he could more nearly visualize how the house was to fit its site. The second report, dated April 18, was no more hopeful:

> Briefly, we cannot recommend the site as suitable, from a structural standpoint, for a building of importance such as that contemplated. The rate of recession of the falls may be extremely slow, but cannot be predicted with any degree of safety . . . we do not consider the boulder suitable for incorporation into the foundation of the building. Of course, there is the possibility, or even a probability, that future deterioration of the rock ledge will not be sufficient to endanger the foundations; but in our opinion there could be no feeling of complete safety and consequently we recommend that the proposed site be not used for any important structure.

(The reports from the engineers stood virtually as a monument to educated caution. Kaufmann eventually accepted them as such, and had them buried behind a stone in the wall east of the dining table.)

Wright traveled to Pittsburgh again in mid-April; he was on his way to give a lecture in Philadelphia and he must have thought it best to reassure Kaufmann before anyone sounded further alarms. And, as usual, he was in need of money. Kaufmann and Dombar met him at the

21. *Taliesin, fall 1937. Wright with (from left) Byron Keeler Mosher, Edgar Tafel and William Wesley Peters. Using the compass in the background is John Lautner.*

railroad station and they all went down to Bear Run. Wright was thinking of using Dombar as his field superintendent; the masonry contractor, Zeller, had been working without supervision. Zeller could recall many years later that as many as 42 men were at work under his control. What they were doing is not clear, besides the quarrying on the hill, but Zeller claimed that Wright admired the sample wall they had built: "He said my pattern was perfect."[4] Near the end of the month, Zeller demolished the old bridge abutments. An engineer from Morris Knowles arrived on April 28 to stake out the new bridge; he simply followed the center line and abutment lines of the old one.[5] The stream must have been very low that spring, and the engineer managed to poke

[4] N. J. Zeller, Uniontown, Pa. Conversation of April 13, 1976.

around beneath the upper waterfall. He reported his observations in an office memorandum of May 6:

> There is a ledge of hard sandstone approximately 5 feet thick at the crest of the falls; beneath it a stratum of soft shale 1 to 2 feet thick; and below the shale more sandstone. Below the top 5-foot ledge, the falls have under-cut a distance of approximately 10 feet, or about to the location of the end of one of the foundation walls of the proposed building.

[5] Robert Venturi's criticism of Wright for not accommodating the automobile at Bear Run is quite beside the point, because the bridge and drive were already there. Nor is the bridge "perpendicular" to the drive, but rather to the stream—as it should be. The drive is about ten feet wide at its narrowest. See Venturi, *Complexity and Contradiction in Architecture* (New York, 1966), p. 58.

Now that Wright was pressed to work out the structure of the house more definitely, he turned to Peters and Glickman. William Wesley Peters had joined the Fellowship at its beginning, when he was only 20 years old and fresh from two years at the Massachusetts Institute of Technology. He was serious, loyal, handsome and so tall that he could not walk through Wright's home entirely at ease, especially not when Wright would say, "Wes, sit down—you're ruining the scale of my architecture!" Peters was one of Wright's favorite apprentices. But one spring morning in 1935 he drove off with a young woman named Svetlana, who was Mrs. Wright's daughter by an earlier marriage; because the Wrights thought she was too young to be getting married, Peters and his bride were estranged from Taliesin for about a year. He missed the early drawings for Fallingwater.

Mendel Glickman was not an apprentice; he was older and already an accomplished architectural engineer. Bob Mosher remembers that when he first arrived at Taliesin in October 1932 it was Glickman who met him and took him in to meet Wright. Glickman and his wife had been there for several months before the Fellowship got under way. They had returned to America in 1931 from Russia, where Glickman, who was born in Vitebsk in 1895 and brought to this country when nine years old, served as the chief American engineer for the construction and production-line development of the first tractor factory in Stalingrad, as it was then called. Glickman did not stay at Taliesin very long—married couples rarely found the communal pattern of life there very satisfactory—but he remained dedicated to Wright, and Wright often called on him. Wright's own training in engineering had been brief. His sense of structure was largely intuitive, like his sympathy for nature—by which indeed his structural ideas were usually nurtured. The danger, of course, was that his ideas would outdistance the means at hand, or enter realms where the "slide-rule engineers," as he called them, would fear to tread.[6]

While the structural calculations were in the hands of Peters and Glickman, work at the site was not proceeding very smoothly. Dombar was not even being paid:

> After a month or so I told Mr. K. that I hadn't been receiving any salary. According to the architect-owner agreement he had been sending supervision money to Taliesin; it was up to them to pay me; I phoned Mr. W., who indicated that to him I still was an "apprentice" and should not have expected to be paid. The Kaufmanns took care of my meals . . . so I tried to

accept Mr. Wright's attitude on the matter. Soon the apprentices at Taliesin were complaining that the "rebel," who had left the Fellowship, was being rewarded with the juicy plum, and so the following month Mr. W. brought out Bob Mosher to take over my duties.

Dombar's weeks during May seem to have been occupied mostly with attempts at getting started. Kaufmann advised Wright on May 6 that plans for the bridge had not arrived, even though Zeller was already at work on the piers. Kaufmann also wondered when he would see the craftsman who was to build his new office: "In another three weeks I am going to be without an office as the furniture in my present office is to be shipped to our New York office. I will be sitting on a keg of nails using a soap box for my desk."

Wright said on May 8 that he was sending the bridge plans. A few days later he wrote Walter J. Hall, a contractor in the Port Allegheny area of northern Pennsylvania, to ask whether the house would interest him; Hall soon accepted the offer, but did not get to Bear Run until July 12. (Zeller liked to say that he lost the contract simply because his wife had him arrested one weekend and told Kaufmann that he could not come to work. But by all accounts the bridge was badly begun; it was rebuilt about a year later.)

The revised working drawings for the house were finished on May 27, and four days later Wright was on his way to Bear Run. He had Edgar Tafel and Bob Mosher with him. Byron Keeler Mosher, the apprentice chosen by Wright to take Dombar's place, was a short and alert young man who worried about his name. He had yellow hair and a quick broad smile, and sometimes Wright called him "Little Sunshine," a name he does not recall with any apparent joy; he did not even like his given name, Byron, and was so intent on being called Bob that he took his diploma from the University of Michigan as "Robert" Keeler Mosher. He has always thought that Wright was especially fond of him because he asked the kind of questions about Wright's architecture that the more fawning apprentices would not dare ask.

Wright, Mosher and Tafel met Kaufmann in Pittsburgh on June 5. At last a contract was signed for the office; Wright and the Fellowship were to build it and to have it furnished by September 15; it was to cost 6000 dollars. Kaufmann could hardly have expected that two more Septembers would go by without his office being finished.

When they arrived at Bear Run, they saw soon enough that the bridge across the stream was not at all right. Some of the stone masonry lacked the character Wright was after—those shifting ledges that could stand as a rough but sophisticated abstraction of the native sedi-

---

[6] Wright, *An Autobiography*, pp. 343, 479. Glickman was a professor of architecture and engineering at the University of Oklahoma, in Norman, from 1949 until his death in 1967. He is buried close to Wright and Eugene Masselink in the Lloyd-Jones family cemetery, across state route 23 from Taliesin.

mentary beds—and the edges of the concrete parapets were poorly modeled. Mosher was more worried, though, about the lay of the land. How, in that wild place, could he find the "datum," or level, for the first floor? The plot plan took note of four boulders on the north side of the stream; one was to be under the living-room floor, virtually a fulcrum on which the house would balance (as one of the most beautiful drawings, a north-south section looking west, made clear [22]). It was Wright's understanding that *this* boulder was Kaufmann's favorite spot for lying in the sun and listening to the falls; he had told some of the apprentices that he was going to put it at the heart of the house, in fact make it the hearth.

Mosher asked Wright about the datum. Wright told him to get through the rhododendron and on top of the boulder; when he got there, Wright told him that now he should know. Up on the boulder, Mosher was not standing much higher than Wright, who was down at the bridge; the roadway of the bridge was set at 1309.5 feet above sea level, and the datum was to be at 1311.7 feet.

Wright's feeling for the site was so keen that the act of crossing the bridge (a span of more than 28 feet) and approaching the entrance of the house (60 feet past the bridge) would always seem an uphill journey into a private territory, even though the entrance (at three steps below the living-room floor) was at an elevation only six inches higher than the bridge roadway [23]. Such was his mastery of the rhythm in horizontal line and plane that, although the chimney mass would rise more than 30 feet above the living-room floor, the house from every point would seem very low to the ground.

Mosher officially began as "clerk of the works" on June 8, although he had already sent his first progress report back to Taliesin on Sunday, the day before. He soon reported that the stone stairway from the east side of the house to the stream was in construction. The steps were not going to lead into the stream, but instead to a small "plunge pool." Kaufmann had asked Wright on April 20 for a change in the plans to incorporate a little reservoir of quiet water. Mosher and Wright continued to corre-

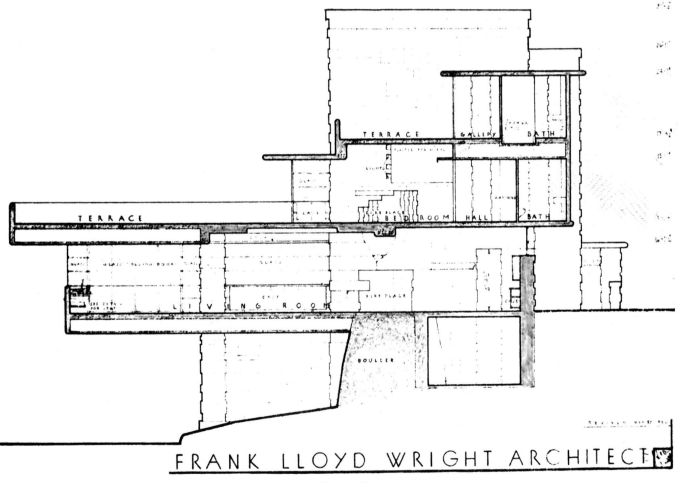

22. *Section of house, looking west.*

23. *East side of house.*

24. *Plunge pool. Bronze sculpture is Jacques Lipchitz's "Mother and Child" of 1941–1945.*

spond about the pool, but the drawing for it was not finished until August 20. Wright fitted it very easily into his scheme of long stone walls [24]. (The plunge is gravity-fed, not from the stream so nearby but from a reservoir east of the highway. The water of the plunge is only 53 inches deep.)

The bridge was finished by the end of June, although not to anyone's satisfaction, and the stone footings were started for three "bolsters," which were to rise from the edge of the stream as if on tiptoe, in support of the cantilevered slab of the first floor [25]. Wright paid no attention to the engineers' recommendation that the footings be widened from two feet to three feet to better resist any battering from a flood, even though the stone piers above, between the living room and the second-story terrace, were to be three feet wide (east-west). He seemed to be more concerned with the shape of the bolsters. At the lower right-hand corner of his first plan-sketch, in September 1935, he had indicated a brusquely stepped-out profile for the bolsters, something like a short flight of stairs turned sideways. In drawings of a few months later, the bolsters were shown as only slightly stepped-out to create horizontal shadow lines.[7] But they were to function simply as vertical supports; because they were not to be walls of stone or wood naturally in sympathy with some horizontal expression, they could receive that sort of emphasis only as decoration, not as an articulation of the pattern of structure. So he finally let the bolsters flare outward without interruption as they rose to curve gently into the floor slab in surfaces shaped by a seven-inch radius. (The bolsters grew from 15 inches wide at the footings to more than three feet wide

[7] The same kind of streamlining would appear very soon in Wright's detailing of the reinforced-concrete columns of the Johnson Administration Building. (A sample column was test-loaded in June 1937.) There he called the column "dendriform" and its capital the "calyx," acknowledging his natural sources of inspiration. The streamlined motif based on horizontal overlaps, stepped out and up, dated back at least to 1922. Lloyd Wright, his eldest son, then working with him, writes in a letter of Jan. 23, 1976, that traditional American clapboarding, "while practical as sheathing, was in the view of my father and myself aesthetically weak and cheap and characterless. So when we were making studies for the Tahoe cabins we indicated a bolder detail . . . overlaps of the siding holding the siding face not pitched—as on the typical milled lapped siding—but vertical, and with the thickness of the wood siding gaining richness and strength structurally as well as visually . . . ." This appeared in much of the exterior of Lloyd Wright's house of 1922 for Martha Taggart; in a balcony of a residence on Olive Hill; in the Tahoe "shore type" cabin and cabin barge "for two" projects of about 1922 and in the first scheme of 1922 for the C. P. Lowes house at Eagle Rock, Calif. Walter Burley Griffin, an assistant of Wright's at the Oak Park studio from 1901 to 1905, used this detail in concrete in a projecting bay of his 1912–1913 house for Joshua G. Melson in Mason City, Ia.

at the floor slab.) This, to Wright's way of thinking, was the supported growing from the support, "somewhat as a tree-branch glides out of its tree trunk"—an expression, though one not easily observed at the site, of the continuity in the material and the structure of the house.[8] The final revised drawing of the bolster detail was finished June 1.

From the way Wright went about his first plan-sketch, and from the spacing of the bolsters, it is apparent that the house was based on a regular system of bays, or what John Lautner remembers as a "horizontal module to suit the rock foundations in the stream." Wright was wonderfully able to use the module as a tool in organizing his planning, rather than as a means toward an easy and academic symmetry (which would make little sense, in any event, because it is not possible at Bear Run to see the south elevation of the house [26] as it appears in drawings). The spaces of the house were generally framed by four nearly equal bays: the west bay reached from the west wall of the kitchen to the west wall of the living room (with Kaufmann's dressing room above, and Edgar Kaufmann, jr.'s, room above that); the two middle bays formed the central space of the living room (the master bedroom above, and a long gallery at the third level); and the east bay defined the skylighted study area, the principal entrance, and stairs (with guest bedroom above). The indication in Wright's first plan-sketch

[8] Wright, *An Autobiography,* p. 341.

25. *Bolsters under first floor.*

26. *House from the southeast, November 1937.*

RIGHT: *27. Beam structure of east living-room terrace, October 1936.*
BELOW: *28. Finished east living-room terrace, November 1937.*

of a fifth bay even farther to the east was already gone in a study for the south elevation, except to the degree that it was expressed by the parapet of the east living-room terrace and by the reach of the loggia eastward from the entrance.

So the south arm of the east living-room terrace, with a floor space measuring almost 24 feet east-west, stretched across two bays in balancing the great span of the doubled bay that formed the central space of the living room. In contrast, the west living-room terrace (its floor measuring 13 feet ten inches east-west) was cantilevered past the line of the west kitchen wall, a subtlety which not only enhanced the drama of the cantilever but also averted any simplistic and monotonous expression of the bay module. The doubled bay in the living room meant that one of the bolsters below the floor would not be expressed, in the south part of the room, by a wall or pier above it. Wright had no intention of sacrificing his freedom to develop space, inside or out, to a structural grid. (Measurements in the house as it was built tend always to the irregular: the horizontal module is about 12 feet, and in the spacing of the horizontal steel members of the window framing there is a vertical module of between 16 and 17 inches.)

At first, Kaufmann must have thought that his new office would be built nearly as scheduled; Wright wrote him on June 15 that although cypress was not regularly in stock, the logs were on the way to Algoma, Wisconsin.

In a few days, he said, he and Manuel (Sandy) Sandoval would be headed north to choose the flitches, or logs, from which the veneers would be cut. Sandoval, a Nicaraguan apprentice of Wright's who was essentially a craftsman, was to be in charge of constructing the office. But on July 23 Wright's secretary wrote Kaufmann that the logs would not arrive in Algoma until July 28. More such delays continued for many months.

But work at Bear Run went ahead; in July the basement was excavated (it was only a small space for the boiler room, some storage shelves and a half-bathroom) and the stone walls were taken up to the level of the first floor. The new contractor, Walter J. Hall, seemed to be a crude and uneducated man, and he was; but having so little to unlearn was perhaps his best recommendation to Wright. Contractors who behaved like "experienced" professionals, Wright thought, would too often obstruct his intentions: they would be too quick to object to any new way of building, and too ready to stick by their mistakes merely to save face.[9] With a comparatively naïve contractor and one of the inexperienced apprentices from Taliesin, Wright hoped, there would at least be more enthusiasm.

Such an arrangement put the apprentice under great pressure, and Mosher was soon aware of the delicacy of his role at Bear Run. Having very little knowledge of construction, he was supposed to "supervise" a very complex and unusual building project. Hall was both clumsy and careless, the labor was mostly local, and Wright was so far away that he could not very often visit the site. (Mosher can recall only about three visits by Wright during the entire term of construction of the main house, and one of Kaufmann's records of payment also shows travel expenses paid to Wright only three times between the summer of 1936 and the fall of 1937; but Wright stopped by a few other times while he was making other trips East. By October 1937, according to Wright's tally, he had been to Pittsburgh 11 times, but he did not always go down to Bear Run.) Kaufmann usually went down to Bear Run on Friday night, for the weekend, to watch how the house was coming along. He appointed his own representative, Carl F. Thumm, who was assistant manager in charge of the store and warehouse buildings. Despite his lame leg, Thumm pecked around the house in a most persistent way. He was experienced in dealing with tradesmen and material suppliers, but he did not get along well with Walter Hall. Nor was he used to Wright or to Wright's kind of working drawings (which were often less than specific), and he held no

29. Steps from living room to stream.

great respect for either. Mosher could see, however, that Thumm would be helpful in expediting the delivery of materials and that he would also serve as a shield between Wright and Kaufmann.

By the first week of August the formwork was under way for the slab of the first floor. Kaufmann was worried about the extent of the cantilever, and not without reason; the slab was going to project 18 feet past the stone piers beneath the bolsters. For reassurance he turned to the Metzger-Richardson Company, a Pittsburgh firm of registered engineers and suppliers of steel for concrete. Metzger-Richardson simply made their own drawings for the reinforcement of the floor slab. The drawings, which were finished on August 10, were not merely shop drawings based on Wright's specifications: "At the time we furnished the steel for these beams," the engineers wrote in a later report, "we put in twice as much steel as was called for on the plans."[10] Mosher particularly remembers the principal reinforcement bars. There were 12 of them, and each was one inch square. The steel arrived at Bear Run on August 15; the floor slab was poured on August 19.

The day the floor was poured two serious mistakes were made: the heavy steel bars were inserted "surrepti-

[9] Wright, *An Autobiography*, pp. 448–450. His discussion of the house on Bear Run is concerned almost entirely with problems of construction and supervision.

[10] Report of June 1, 1937, by the Metzger-Richardson Co. to Edgar J. Kaufmann, p. 4.

tiously," as Mosher puts it, and no one was mindful of the slight deflection that could be expected in any cantilever; the floor was poured at true level instead of being canted to compensate for later deflection. The first of these mistakes caused hard feelings, the second resulted in the slightly drooping lines that worried Kaufmann for the rest of his life.

The one-inch-square bars were placed in the four major floor beams, running north-south; the beams were two feet wide and the concrete joists between them, spaced four feet apart, were four inches thick. To accommodate the hatch to the stream the easternmost beam had to be eccentric; it swung farther to the east in a semicircular detour and it was thickened to three feet wide to support the cantilevered east terrace [27, 28]. (Kaufmann continued to wonder why the hatch and hanging steps were needed at all; it seemed an extravagant complication, with the steps not really leading anywhere. As late as April 2, 1937, Wright sent a telegram to Kaufmann to argue that the hatch would have no meaning without the intimate relation to the stream by way of the steps—that the steps were absolutely necessary from every standpoint [29, 30]. Edgar Kaufmann, jr., stood with Wright in defending the stairs as being essential to the spatial rhythm of the house. A second, smaller flight of hanging steps, for the specific purpose of giving direct access from the second story to the stone steps of the plunge pool [31], required a cut through the second-floor slab.)

When they came to live in the house, the Kaufmanns found the hatch to function very well as a way of ventilating the living room [32, 33]. Yet the area of the hatch was more basically an aesthetic development—one that the historian Talbot Hamlin was quick to call "perhaps

30. Steps to stream, November 1937. View from under bridge.

the climax of the whole house."[11] There, as Edgar Kaufmann, jr., has pointed out, a complex and transparent shaft of space (the channel defined by the stairwell, hatch, surrounding parapet, glass walls and perforated roof slab) opened the east corner of the living room to light below and light above, and to horizontal vistas as well: in that sense, the space counterbalanced the dense chimney mass at the opposite corner of the room. In turn, the chimney mass abutted a continuous shaft of windows —which lighted not the stairs of the house, as one might reasonably assume, but the kitchen and two west bedrooms above it [34]. The hanging stairs opposed the flow of water over the falls, a delicate gesture of balance. The entire house would be a matter of balance: between terrace and anchoring mass, between the outdoors and a family's habitation, between outflowing space and close sanctuary. A glance through the hatch could reveal how the house took its place above the stream. The waxed flags of the living-room floor had the same color and the same texture as the glistening bedrock of the stream. Wright liked to think of glass in terms of "limpid surfaces playing the same part . . . that water plays in the landscape." And the hatch of course suggested a ship, and all the freedom in space which a ship signifies to the romantic imagination.[12]

Two days before the first-floor structure was poured, Thumm asked Metzger-Richardson to consider how the

second-story west terrace might be changed into a "small diving pool." Drawings for the change were sent to Kaufmann's Store within a few days, but Mosher could not keep silent: he alerted Wright, who insisted that the pool stay under the house and below the east terrace of the living room. Mosher had reported on July 4 that Kaufmann wanted to widen the stone steps to the little plunge (some would be less than three feet wide, although the bottom step of the much more symbolic stairs from the hatch would be eight feet wide), but Wright now directed that the steps be left as they were [35]. He also wrote that the stone bath by the main entrance should be outdoors, where fresh flowers might be kept until they could be arranged throughout the house, and where the clients could dip their feet without wetting the entry floor [36]. The entrance loggia would be one and seven-tenths of a foot lower than the living-room floor, a narrow and usually dark space [37] which would lead to

[11] Talbot F. Hamlin, "F.L.W.—An Analysis," *Pencil Points,* 19 (March 1938), p. 138.

[12] Wright, "In the Cause of Architecture: Standardization, The Soul of the Machine," *Architectural Record,* 61 (June 1927), p. 480. The house is a rare instance of streamlining in direct relation to a stream. Long before Art Moderne stylisms popularly celebrated speed, Wright used his own streamlining to strip away irrelevant detail and decoration, and to express freedom, quiet and repose. In *The Disappearing City* (New York, 1932), p. 18, he attacked the overgrown city as "the dam across the stream flowing toward freedom." He wrote that his "Ocatillo" cabins in Arizona were "like ships coming down the mesa" (*An Autobiography,* p. 310). And, at the end of his life, he said of the Guggenheim Museum building in New York, "You will feel it as a curving wave that never breaks" (*Life,* Nov. 2, 1959, p. 81).

31. *Hanging steps from second story.*

ABOVE: *32. Hatch to stream and doors to east living-room terrace, November 1937.*
OPPOSITE: *33. Hatch opened, November 1937.*

34. Shaft of windows for kitchen and two west bedrooms.

the left, then up to the great living space and its glass walls welcoming the beauty of the glen.

The stone masonry was taken up to the level of the second story by August 20. Thumm, in his fussy way, wrote Mosher on August 26 to record the fact that he had already given him a tracing of "our engineering idea as to the swimming pool" off Kaufmann's dressing room. Evidently Mosher had not yet received Wright's letter. "It was the intention that you develop the architectural features of the pool and return your suggestions so that we may have the engineer develop same structurally," Thumm wrote. "Please be advised the reinforcing steel for the second floor is being held up at this point until a decision is arrived at." Wright's mandate soon carried the day, but Mosher's position had become ever more precarious.

By early in September, Wright had heard about the heavy steel bars in the first-floor slab, and had called Mosher back to Taliesin. "I was in disgrace," Mosher remembers. Edgar Tafel was sent to take his place. Tafel, another of the original group of apprentices at Taliesin, was energetic, fun-loving and fond of the piano (although he played it much to the displeasure of Gurdjieff, the mystic friend of Mrs. Wright). He recalls arriving at Bear Run when the formwork was in place for the second floor. The slab was poured on September 16; the finished floor level was to be nine feet two and one-half inches above that of the first floor. The depth of the floor structure itself, however, would be two feet one and one-half inches (from top of flags to soffits), or the same as in the first floor. So the ceiling height of the living room would be only seven feet one inch, except in special places of recessed lighting.

Because these indentations would be toward the center and the back of the room, the lower ceiling plane near the brighter walls of glass at the perimeter would give a certain velocity to the outward flow of space, toward broad horizontal vistas. Four principal bearing points defined the central indentation of the ceiling: the two stone piers toward the south side of the living room, the stone wall that screened the entry from the dining area, and the north part of the chimney mass. Edgar Kaufmann, jr., has pointed out that the space below this central indentation served as a common area between the more particularized places of the living space: the dining table at the north, an area for music near the entry (where a Capehart record player was built in), the writing desk and bookshelves near the hatch to the stream, and the built-in seats at the outer walls of the room. Thus the space of the living room, measuring more than 48 feet north-south and more than 38½ feet east-west, was organized and articulated and yet entirely free. Finally, the stepped space of the ceiling echoed the stepped

ABOVE: 35. Stone steps to plunge pool. BELOW: 36. Stone foot-bath by main entry.

massing of the entire house—another "graceful reflex."

Two extensions of the second-floor slab became trellises. The row of trellis beams at the east corner of the living room formed eight rectangular windows in the roof, four open and outdoors and the other four glazed as skylights above the bookshelves and writing desk [38]. "Ceilings will often become as window-walls," Wright wrote.[13] The trellis beams were spaced 39 inches apart, and the regular pattern of spaces between them mediated subtly between indoors and out. In section, the beams were slightly wedge-shaped; they echoed the shape of the bolsters beneath the first floor. Turned to the morning sun, the trellis cast patterns of sun splashes across the living-room floor. The second row of trellis beams served a more structural purpose; the beams anchored part of the second-floor slab by crossing the drive-

[13] Wright, *An Autobiography*, p. 340.

way to tie into the rock cliff at the north [39]. Two of the 12 beams arced around the trunks of trees close by the walls of the house [40].

Tafel had to remove one tree to make way for the cantilevered west-bedroom terrace, which, in a sense, was also a lateral extension of the second floor (even though it was six steps, or more than three feet, above it). But there were three more trees that Wright wanted left free to rise through the terrace, tying the house to its site. The structure of the terrace slab was to consist of only a single longitudinal beam (18 inches wide) and six smaller transverse beams. Three of the transverse beams keyed directly into a boulder at the driveway; the reinforcement bars were bent down into lead anchors in the rock. In order to save the three trees, box-like appendages were attached to the transverse beams [41, 42].

Having abandoned his attempt to change the west-bedroom terrace into a swimming pool, Kaufmann now

37. Entrance loggia.

proposed another change. On a drawing sent from Bear Run back to Wright someone noted that Kaufmann had been sitting on the hill and studying the construction of the terrace, and had suggested that the north part of the parapet be ended about nine feet from the west corner, to keep the terrace from looking "boxy, floppy and not at all strong." Wright responded directly on the drawing: "What's wrong with boxy?" Then, more seriously: "Parapet must continue or entire construction will look disintegrated.—F. Ll. W." He won again.

In the fall of 1936, construction lagged behind the schedule Hall was supposed to be following, but Kaufmann's enthusiasm was far from flagging. The slow process of construction itself was celebrated by frequent photographs; a series taken on October 21 has survived as a comprehensive record [43–45].

The third floor would be 17 feet eight and one-half inches above the first, with much of the floor structure now thinned to only eight and one-half inches in depth. The slab was folded for greater strength and for a variation of the ceiling height in the second-story bedrooms; as in the living room, the change in ceiling inflected the space toward the glass walls and the outdoors. (It amounted to a drop from a generous seven feet nine and one-half inches on the north side of each bedroom to six feet four and one-half inches on the south, near the doors and windows.) The roofs would be seven-inch slabs, and they would be extended as floating planes to soften the light, induce a sense of shelter and express again the freedom Wright believed implicit in the horizontal line.

Very soon after the second floor was poured, cracks appeared in the parapets. Kaufmann was worried, and Tafel warned Wright about Thumm studying the cracks and saying he would "figure it all out." Cracks from shrinkage could have been averted, Wright wrote Kaufmann on November 2, if there had been expansion

38. East corner of living room with trellis skylights, November 1937.

joints above the points of bearing, though joints in the faces of cantilevered masses would have looked absurd. A jointed cantilever would be an anomaly, Wright said: no one would be able to realize that the floor beam was the actual support.[14] He tried to put Kaufmann at ease. All concrete structures were expected to have cracks, he wrote; cracks would weaken concrete not at all, and though they could be hidden they would go on working forever. Wright also demanded to be told about Thumm's role at Bear Run, and he hastened to make little of him. (In other communications, Tafel has recalled, Wright misspelled Thumm's name in about as many ways as he could think of.)

[14] He in fact used such expansion joints in the upper walls of the Imperial Hotel, but expressly to combat the racking movements of earthquakes. See Robert Kostka, "Frank Lloyd Wright in Japan," *Prairie School Review*, III (3rd quarter, 1966), p. 17.

Kaufmann was not so easily convinced. Wright soon called Mendel Glickman, and they both traveled to Bear Run. According to Tafel, Glickman once confessed that "maybe" he had forgotten to calculate the "negative moment," an engineers' term for the amount of droop, or frown-like bending, of a beam because of stresses above its point of support. Glickman stayed at Bear Run about a week, his wife recalled not long ago, and when he came home he said everything was satisfactory to both Wright and himself. But evidently not to Kaufmann.

Hall had taken samples of the concrete he used in the first-floor slab, and in his crude way had stored them in fruit jars; but because his performance was already in question, and justly so, Wright sent a plan for making test cuts in the floor joists and parapet. Mosher, now back at Bear Run—Tafel had been called to Taliesin to help with the preliminary drawings for the Johnson Adminis-

39. Second-floor trellis beams tying into rock cliff.

40. *Trellis beam curved to accept tree trunk.*

LEFT: *41. Transverse beams of west-bedroom terrace, December 1936.* BELOW: *42. View from finished west-bedroom terrace, November 1937.* OPPOSITE: *43. Formwork and cantilevers, October 1936.*

LEFT: 44. *Second floor, northwest corner, October 1936.* BELOW: 45. *View from bridge, October 1936.*

46. House in the snow, December 1936.

tration Building—was directed to cut into the slab as delicately as possible with a pneumatic drill and take sample cubes near the most visible fracture. He sent the cubes away for laboratory analysis, and it is his recollection that the report confirmed the aggregate to be perfectly strong. (On the other hand, Edgar Kaufmann, jr., remembers that when openings were made in the concrete many years later, to ventilate the slabs, pure sand sometimes poured out. The openings also revealed that some of the insulation in the terrace floors had been sealed in while wet, and had rotted the subflooring. This had caused what seemed to be "leaks" throughout the house.)

If he professed not to be worried about the cracks in the concrete, Wright nevertheless had misgivings about the structural relation of the parapets to the floor slabs. He thought the parapets were adding dead weight to the extremities of the cantilevers, rather than helping to support them; and he seems to have blamed the weight of the parapets for the signs of negative moment in the second-floor slab at the east side of the house. The next time, he wrote, "parapets will carry the floors—or better still we will know enough to make the two work together as one, as I originally intended."[15]

(John H. Howe thinks that the parapets did work in continuity with the floor structure to the extent that they stiffened the outer edges, much like the sides of a shallow box; Peters and Edgar Kaufmann, jr., agree. It is Tafel's opinion that in Glickman's calculations the only part of the parapets that acted as a stiffening beam was the lowest part, across the depth of the floor slab itself [see 22], and that the slender steel bars in the parapet walls were of no help. Mosher recalls sitting by Wright's side

while Wright battled pneumonia and a very high fever, an illness he suffered about the time the Johnson Administration Building was being finished, in the winter of 1938–1939, and hearing him mumble about Fallingwater being "too heavy." Wright told his apprentices in later years that he would rather have had the parapets designed as truss beams, to carry the floor slabs.)

By the end of 1936, the shell of the house on Bear Run seemed under a palpable shadow of doubts [46]. On December 2, Thumm wrote Metzger-Richardson that Kaufmann had found a "third check" in the second-story parapet wall that ran at a right angle to the master-bedroom terrace. He wrote them again on December 11, asking them to "start at once" an investigation of the structure of the house, and to suggest remedies. The engineers had already been to Bear Run three days earlier, for the first of what would seem to be an endless series of inspections. They found cracks in five places: in the eccentric first-floor beam at the stairwell to the stream, in the stairwell parapet, in the first-floor beam at the opposite side of the house, in the joists of the east living-room terrace and in the parapet of the master bedroom terrace. The cracks extended through the members, they reported, and would have to be considered structural. They blamed most of the cracks on excessive stress, but said that those in the second-story parapet, which worried Kaufmann the most, were due to the deflection of the first floor.

The remedies suggested by the engineers were all the same: an extension of direct vertical supports under all the cantilever beams and joists deemed to be overstressed.[16] Such a prospect threatened to compromise the very nature of the house on Bear Run.

[15] Wright, in the *Architectural Forum*, 68 (Jan. 1938), p. 36.

[16] The first six months of inspections, tests and sightings are reviewed in the engineers' report of June 1, 1937. A copy is in the Avery Library.

Chapter IV
FINISHING THE HOUSE: 1937

Despite the problems at Bear Run—the delays, misunderstandings and signs of structural stress—Kaufmann seemed to have unbounded confidence; in a telegram to Wright on January 6, 1937, he was eager to share it:

All is well. Sandoval with helper arrived this morning. Office will be constructed according to your latest plan. Cheer up, all difficulties must be overcome. Anxiously awaiting your solution as to what should be done because of the checks. Also your scheme to take the place of masonry materials [in the subflooring] and your authorization to start laying the floors in certain parts of the house. These solutions are all necessary for us to continue to work during the winter. . . . With all the difficulties it still remains a noble structure.

One of Mosher's most vivid impressions from his first winter on Bear Run was of the snow; not only its beauty ("Bear Run is like a Hiroshige snow-print," he wrote Kaufmann on February 4) but also its weight, gathered along the edges of the terrace above the living room, where Hall had stacked bags of sand and cement near his construction shed [47]. Mosher thought the cantilever was being subjected to the greatest possible stress, and he thought it an especially stupid act on Hall's part. Perhaps it was; but the engineers from the Metzger-Richardson Company were periodically loading the cantilevers to test what they called the "stability" of the structure. With the approval of Carl Thumm, the first tests were conducted on January 6 and 13. To load the terraces the engineers used 94-pound sacks of cement, 94-pound sacks of sand and five-foot lengths of cast-iron pipe (each weighing 65 pounds). The purpose of the loading was to measure the deflections.

The engineers had already warned Kaufmann in December that the stresses in the roof above the guest's terrace exceeded "the allowable by a wide margin." Wright had not expected the roof to require any direct support, but now he offered a sketch showing a row of reinforcement bars extending through a vertical concrete panel with what Edgar Tafel recalls as "a 'moon' window in the middle of it." The idea struck the Kaufmanns as excessively fanciful and Oriental, and they thought the motif related to nothing else in the house (though perhaps Wright considered the "window" to be a reflex of the various arcs in the house). Thumm simply noted that the steel rods would be exposed, and he asked the engineers to "please consider whether or not this type of design will have any structural value . . . ." After various suggestions, Wright deleted the concrete element and settled for additional rods encased in steel channels. Finally, these were removed and a stone wall was built as the support. It was only four feet nine inches long, and one and a half feet wide; it was not conspicuous, but if noticed at all it held the eye [48]. Here was a stone support, between concrete slabs, which was not continued on down to the ground. It seemed to be hovering, and was in fact carried by the terrace floor, which in turn was secured by the trellis beams that tied into the cliff behind the drive. "It just didn't belong, and we all knew it," Tafel said not long ago.

The engineers also worried about the opposite side of the house, the west-bedroom terrace. In one of the changes he had made between his first sketches and the working drawings, Wright extended the cantilever slab even farther: the terrace floor measured 28 feet five inches east-west [49]. After the engineers calculated the stresses on the principal cantilever beam and found them greatly in excess of the "allowable," they recommended that a stone wall be extended under the beam to reduce its span from 16 to eight feet. Thumm noted on January 4 that the four-foot stone pier was in place; the terrace was test-loaded two days later, and the engineers were satisfied. Wright, when he discovered it later, was not. No one had asked him about the wall, so he did not tell anyone when he ordered Mosher to take out the top course of stones. Edgar Kaufmann, jr., recalls his father finally confessing to Wright: "If you've not noticed it . . . there can't be anything very bad about it, architecturally." Wright then walked with Kaufmann to below the

47. Cantilevers, December 1936.

terrace. "When I was here last month," he said, "I ordered the top layers of stone removed. Now, the terrace has shown no sign of failing. Shall we take down the extra four feet of wall?"[1]

Work at Bear Run went slowly during January. Hope's Windows, Inc., of Jamestown, New York, was supplying the steel sash (made to order from stock sections), and the sash for the three-story channel of windows was in place by the second week of the month. Discussions were under way with Hope's on how to fabricate the hatch to the stream, which would involve horizontally telescoping

[1] Edgar Kaufmann, jr., "Twenty-five Years of the House on the Waterfall," *L'architettura—cronache e storia*, 82 (Aug. 1962, p. 41.

units [see 33]. So many other details remained to be decided, or clarified, that Hall traveled to Taliesin for further instructions. Wright had originally specified two-inch gypsum plank for the subflooring, with interlinings of asphaltum building paper; but now he decided to use redwood two-by-fours instead. (Edgar Tafel recalls the redwood being chosen to reduce the weight in the floors; Edgar Kaufmann, jr., believes the decision had more to do with damping of sound transmissions, and a letter of January 13 from Thumm to E. J. Kaufmann is indeed concerned entirely with sound transmissions. When the stones of the terrace floors were taken up many years later to rid the subflooring of the moisture that was causing apparent leaks, the redwood timbers were found

48. Fallingwater, November 1937.

badly rotted.) Wright provided Hall a memorandum on various finishing details, with even a tiny sketch showing how to curve the mortar of the one-inch joints between stones in the floors. The roofs were to blend in with the parapets by having a thin coat of cream-to-light-gold-colored gravel spread over the final coat of asphalt.

Mosher reported to Kaufmann on February 4 that he was very busy making diagrams for the woodwork, which would be in black-walnut veneer. Kaufmann had left Pittsburgh on January 11 for seven weeks in Palm Beach, Florida, and in Mexico. He responded on February 10:

In spite of having had a very pleasant and restful holiday, my thoughts have been daily, almost hourly, with the work in Bear Run which has become part of me and a part of my life and one hates to be separated until the work has been completed to everyone's satisfaction. When completed it should be a credit to all. Do not forget in drawing the details for furniture and woodwork that this is not a town house but a mountain lodge and should have that feeling in its furnishings . . .

A few days later Kaufmann wrote a letter of encouragement to Hall: "I can quite understand your reaction to Taliesin but as I have always said and believe that in spite of all that has occurred, when it is finished, it is going to be an achievement. I know you will be proud having had a hand in putting it together."

Long before it was finished, the house began to attract attention. Henry S. Churchill, a New York architect and planner, photographed it on October 23, 1936, before

49. *Cantilevered west-bedroom terrace.*

there was a third story.[2] In March 1937, the *St. Louis Post-Dispatch* published in color the rendering Wright had made with John Howe standing at his side. When interviewed, Wright gave the impression, quite exaggerated, that he had directed Kaufmann's attention to the waterfall site, saying, "You love this waterfall, don't you? Then why build your house miles away, so you will have to walk to it? Why not live intimately with it, where you can see and hear it and feel it with you all the time?" He also said the house would cost 45,000 dollars and that its concrete surfaces would be finished, probably, with gold leaf—the quiet gold of Japanese screens.[3]

He was overly sanguine on both counts. By the end of 1937 the costs would total nearly 75,000 dollars. More than 22,000 dollars would be spent from 1938 through 1941 for further finishing and changes in the lighting and hardware. The guest wing and servants' quarters, begun and almost finished in 1939, would cost almost 50,000 dollars more. Probably these sums include payment for

the services of Thumm and some other store employees, such as A. E. Vitaro, the store architect, who made certain shop drawings. The wage scale at Bear Run, Tafel can recall, was 35 cents an hour for common laborers, 70 cents for skilled, 75 for carpenters and 85 for masons. Wright gave Kaufmann just about all the house he could get away with, and certainly far more than the "waterfall cottage" originally discussed. On the other hand, his fees were rather modest; they came to only 8000 dollars.[4]

Mosher likes to recall how gold leaf was written into the specifications. Kaufmann soon objected; it sounded extravagant, and out of character for a "mountain lodge." Wright managed to demur as long as possible. He was fond of the idea. Mosher had written in August 1936 to ask whether any other type of "foil" might be suitable for the concrete surfaces. Wright soon asked a supplier for

[2] Churchill (1893–1962) may have heard about the house directly from Edgar Kaufmann, jr., whom he knew. Eight of his photographs are now in the Avery Library. In "Notes on Frank Lloyd Wright," *Magazine of Art*, 41 (Feb. 1948), p. 64, he wrote of Fallingwater: "There is daring and beauty in the concrete of Bear Run; it is married to masonry—the cut-stone of the structure and the rock of the river."

[3] Max Putzel, "A House That Straddles a Waterfall," *St. Louis Post-Dispatch* Sunday Magazine, March 21, 1937, pp. 1, 7.

[4] A copy of the capital-investment accounting undertaken after Edgar J. Kaufmann's death in 1955 is now in the Avery Library. Wright was not interested only in serving wealthy clients. In 1906 he designed "A Fireproof House for $5,000" for publication in the April 1907 issue of the *Ladies' Home Journal*. Broadacre City was intended to accommodate all classes of society, although it had a distinctly middle-class flavor. His house for Herbert Jacobs, commissioned in August 1936 and finished in 1937 near Madison, Wis., cost only about 5500 dollars, including the architect's fee. His design of a house for a family with 5000 to 6000 dollars in annual income was published in *Life*, Sept. 26, 1938, pp. 60–61. "The house of moderate cost," Wright wrote in *An Autobiography*, p. 489, "is not only America's major architectural problem but the problem most difficult for her major architects."

50. *Living room, looking toward south side.*

price quotations on gold leaf and on aluminum leaf, but not until March 1937 did he suggest to Kaufmann that a sample of mica be tested, since gold leaf was prohibitive and because aluminum leaf might deteriorate after a year unless it was heavily lacquered. A mica-white finish was tested, and although Kaufmann at first did not like it, he later became enthusiastic. Presumably it was more silver than white, a color (or noncolor) that Wright assiduously avoided as being not of the earth, barrenly virginal and alien to the sensuous warmth he sought in colors as well as in textures. In place of the gold leaf, Wright was after something comparable to "the sere leaves of the rhododendron," though in fact the leaves are green through every season. Finally, late in August, it was decided to use a waterproof cement paint called "Cemelith," from Super Concrete Emulsions, Ltd., in Los Ange-les. The order came to 1340 pounds, and the coloring was what Kaufmann called light ochre. How could Wright have seriously proposed gold leaf? Mosher remembers that he thought the humidity from the falls would eventually cause a soft patina; such a quiet and autumnal gold could have been at home in the colors of the forest.[5]

Whatever difficulties they had experienced, Wright could thank Kaufmann for the courage to build the house

[5] Thus the effect would have been far different from the showy sort of fantasy in much Art Deco and Art Moderne gold-leafed ornamentation. Wright's affection for gold surfaces (as for streamlining) was of long standing. He installed Japanese screens at Taliesin and in the Barnsdall house in Los Angeles. He used gold foil on the mortar joints of the Martin house in Buffalo, the Imperial Hotel in Tokyo and the Henry J. Allen house in Wichita—not only to emphasize the horizontal lines but also to visually lighten the masonry masses: gold leaf at Bear Run could have functioned in those ways also.

OPPOSITE: *51. Shaft of windows opened at corner, with floor slabs beveled to meet glazing bars, November 1937.* LEFT: *52. Corner windows in bathroom of master bedroom.* BELOW: *53. Glass into stone.*

at all and for his sympathy for its essential character. Kaufmann was not a passive man and not a passive client; he did not hesitate to make suggestions. If they made sense to Wright, they were freely accepted. One was the little plunge pool. Although intended simply for bathing before breakfast, its captive and quiet water became an aesthetic nuance, the counterpoint to the swift water of the stream. Kaufmann contributed two other characteristic details as the house was being closed in.

On the stream side of the house, cantilever construction relieved the walls of any structural duty (except for the four steel posts in the south bank of living-room windows [50] that helped support the master-bedroom terrace). Thus free, the walls could dissolve into glass, to open the interior to ever-changing vistas across the glen. Wright relished plate glass as a modern material—"the crystal held by the steel as the diamond is held in its setting of gold"[6]—which, in its transparency, might serve to counterweight the masses of ancient stone along the north side of the house. He used the steel sash to create counterrhythms, some horizontal and some vertical, and to assert the freedom in cantilever construction by denying the slightest hint of traditional post-and-beam struc-

[6] Wright, "The Meaning of Materials—Glass," *Architectural Record,* 64 (July 1928), p. 12.

ture: the vertical members were toward the center of the window walls, the horizontal members at the corners. In many of the corners the window glass was mitred and butted; such "wrap-around" windows, he wrote in 1935, were "originally a minor outward expression of the interior folded plane."[7] At seven corners where there seemed to be posts—in the kitchen and two bedrooms above it, at the east corner of the stairwell to the stream, in the bathroom off the master bedroom, in the guest bedroom and at the north corner of the second-story stair landing—the windows were small casements which swung out from both sides [51, 52] to surprise the eye by revealing no vertical support at all.[8]

But the prospect for those places where glass would meet the ragged profiles of stonework was not so happy; Wright thought that special (and probably awkward) framing members would be needed. Kaufmann was the first to suggest that the glass be run directly into caulking channels, or chases, in the stone [53]. Without the boundary of a final framing member, and with this complete interpenetration, the character of each material could be enhanced by contrast with the other.

Another rough and irregular surface belonged to the boulder that protruded through the living-room floor to form the hearth. Wright intended to have it trimmed flush with the floor as soon as the floor was paved with flags. Mosher can remember Kaufmann studying the boulder one weekend, then telling him to leave it be, free to rise above the floor. And he can remember Wright's delight when he discovered what Kaufmann had suggested: "Count one for you, E. J.," Wright said.[9] The boulder stretched from the chimney mass almost seven feet into the room, and at points reached nearly ten inches above the floor level. Rough and potent in its testimony to the site, the hearth became one of the most engaging details anywhere in the house, and a perfect witness to Wright's principle that "it is in the nature of any organic building to grow from its site, come out of

the ground into the light—the ground itself held always as a component basic part of the building itself."[10]

Part of the boulder also protruded through the southeast corner of the kitchen floor, and the flag paving stones everywhere suggested the rock cliffs and the bedrock of the stream. Indoors, the flags were sealed and waxed, but the boulder was not. It came through the floor like the dry top of a boulder peering above the stream waters [54]. Mosher remembers how he selected the flags so the joints would seem to continue beneath the glass doors, to merge indoors and out.

The paving of the floors went slowly. Hall reported that it was going to proceed "full force" on February 22, but on April 5 he reported that the floors still were not entirely finished. Meanwhile, even he had got some inkling of the problem of too much weight; he made his own test loadings on March 22, and his measurements (whether accurate or not), could only have increased Kaufmann's anxiety. Hall said the terrace by the hatch deflected two and three-eighths inches, or half an inch more than when the props were temporarily removed late in 1936, and that the streamside corner of the west living-room terrace deflected two and one-fourth inches, or more than an inch farther than it had three months before. Metzger-Richardson returned to Bear Run on May 21—by then the floors were entirely finished—to compare the deflections due to the total dead load with the sightings taken during the previous test loadings. They confirmed that the greatest deflections were in the living-room terraces, although at no point did a deflection exceed one and five-sixteenths inches. In their "final" report, signed by F. L. Metzger, the senior partner, and submitted on June 1, they reached a conclusion by now all too familiar to Kaufmann:

> The calculated stresses in the structure do not fall within the limits of those proscribed [sic] by accepted engineering practice. From this standpoint, therefore, the structure does not have a satisfactory factor of safety, or what might be termed reserve strength. We believe the recommendations we made from time to time, regarding the extension of supports at different points, should be carried out.

For almost 20 years Kaufmann had engineers travel down to Bear Run to measure the deflections. They plotted their record on graph paper; the number of points on which they took readings grew from 14 to 35. The climate and the nature of the house meant that it would always be slightly in motion. Wright demonstrated that

[7] *Frank Lloyd Wright on Architecture*, ed. Frederick Gutheim (New York, 1941), p. 181. This kind of continuity in glass appeared as early as 1924 in his house for Samuel Freeman in Los Angeles. His spacing of the horizontal sash members in the house on Bear Run at 16 to 17 inches apart approximated the normal spacing of (vertical) studs in wood-frame houses—again subverting traditional construction.

[8] Drop-out corner windows had already appeared in Wright's house for Malcolm Willey, in Minneapolis—not in imitation of mitred-glass corners, but as an alternative way of escaping ordinary construction and its inhibition of flowing space. The windows in the Willey house presented "unobstructed space without even a thin post for support," Lewis Mumford noted in *The New Yorker*, Feb. 12, 1938, p. 59. Gerrit Rietveld in 1924 had devised a "disappearing" corner by displacing a steel post in the upper story of his house for Mrs. Schröder, in Utrecht; see pp. 124–125 of Paul Overy, *De Stijl* (London, 1969).

[9] One of Wright's sons, not having seen the house, assumed that the boulder had been "sheered flat." See John Lloyd Wright, *My Father Who Is On Earth* (New York, 1946), p. 124.

OPPOSITE ABOVE: *54. Boulder at living-room hearth.* OPPOSITE BELOW: *55. Metal shelves above dining table.*

[10] Wright, *An Autobiography*, p. 338.

the extension of the wall under the west-bedroom terrace was not necessary; after that, Kaufmann refused to extend the supports as recommended by the engineers. He stood fast by the house and, except for the sagging roof above the guest's terrace and the sagging trellis above the east living-room terrace, it stood fast by him.

Toward the end of March, Hall worried about the paint Wright specified for the steel sash and all the other metal details, the stair hangers and railings, the fireplace grates and various ornamental touches, and the zinc planter by the hatch—a delightful detail added by Wright in a drawing sent to Hope's on December 2, 1936. It was to be Duco, and Hall was afraid that he would need an expert with a gun to apply it (although, even in the 1920s, advertisements showed Duco being applied to furniture with brushes). Mosher remembers that Wright asked the Du Pont Company, in Wilmington, Delaware, to mix the paint to a "Cherokee red," which was what Wright called the hue of an Indian pot he sent along as a guide. It was typical that Wright would choose a modern product to convey primal associations: red as an earth color, red as·the color of the life force (the notion that he attributed to Timiriazev) and, as Edgar Kaufmann, jr., has observed, red as a sign of the heat entailed in the working of metals.[11]

For two of the metal details the drawings were finished on May 26: the living-room shelves and the spherical kettle by the living-room fireplace. The streamlined shelves might appear to be all too typical of 1930s styling, but in fact they performed three ornamental functions related specifically to the character of the house [55]. They echoed the rock ledges and the concrete cantilevers. By turning their corners in arcs they reinforced another motif of the house. And in coursing along the upper wall from the stone pier at the southwest to the dining area at the north they modulated the transition from wall to ceiling, and from stone to concrete.

The kettle was a more curious detail, conceived by Wright as a way to heat wine over an open fire, and thus again to celebrate the primitive nature of the hearth. It is about 22 inches in diameter, and it was fashioned in Scottdale, Pennsylvania, from cast iron three-eighths of an inch thick. But it could hardly perform its ostensible function: Edgar Kaufmann, jr., remembers the kettle being used only once, and then after a wine punch had already been heated in the kitchen. The sphere swings on a welded crane (once more, the theme of the cantilever) and is at rest in a semicircular niche in the stone wall

ABOVE LEFT: 56. *Wine kettle at hearth.* BELOW LEFT: 57. *Detail of stairs to stream.* OPPOSITE ABOVE: 58. *West-balcony staircase.* OPPOSITE BELOW: 59. *Stairs to servants' quarters of guest wing.*

[56]. Wright changed the plan of the back wall of the
fireplace so that it too became semicircular, in answer to
the arc of the parapet around the stairwell to the stream.
Lesser arcs would appear in the stair hangers, the edges
of the treads [57], the stairs from the guest's terrace
down to the east living-room terrace and in details of the
furniture.

Throughout the house the steps and stairs would serve
not only as passages but also as reflections of the cascad-
ing character of the site. Nowhere would the idea of a
cascade be more forcefully expressed than in the west-
balcony stairs, from the third-story bedroom (later
changed into a study) to the west-bedroom terrace [58].
Here the deliberate stepping of the concrete staircasing
condensed a motif which would soon be reflected elsewhere, particularly in the guest wing [59] and in the
covered walk which led down to the main house. The
stairs indoors were as concentrated as the stairs outdoors
were dispersed; they gathered near the entry, and were
accessible by a series of turns to the right [60]. Just as
the entry was set three steps below the living-room floor,
the second-story landing was three steps below the
second floor. At the second-story landing the space
became extraordinarily complex. Simultaneously it gave
onto steps up to the guest's bedroom [61]; to a glass
door which led outside and then either down to the
plunge pool and east living-room terrace or up to the
guest's terrace [62]; to steps up to the hall which served
the other second-story rooms, or on up to the third story
[63]; and, later, to the bridge which would cross the
drive and connect with the covered walkway [64].
Reflexes of the arc would appear in the leading steps and
in the parapet at the stairwell.

By comparison to the floor space of the living room,
the bedrooms were rather small, but they were intended
to function virtually as antechambers to their respective
terraces [65], which in every instance offered much more
space.[12] Wright thought that screened beds could be
used on the terraces, and Kaufmann even approached a

[11] In writing of his early years in Adler & Sullivan's offices atop
the Auditorium Tower, Chicago, Wright recalled how "the red
glare of the Bessemer steel converters to the south of Chicago
thrilled me as the pages of the Arabian Nights used to do—with a
sense of terror and romance." See *Architectural Record*, 63 (April
1928), p. 350. Wright chose bricks of "Cherokee red" for the
Hanna house in Palo Alto, Calif., and in the Johnson Administration
Building, where he had the aluminum chairs painted the same hue.
[12] The master bedroom, 14' 11" (E-W) × 17', is 255 sq. ft.;
its terrace, 685 sq. ft. Kaufmann's room, 12' 2" × 17' 5", is 210
sq. ft.; the west-bedroom terrace, 455 sq. ft. The guest bedroom,
11' 5" × 15' 1", is 172½ sq. ft.; its terrace, 273 sq. ft. The
third-story bedroom, 11' 4" × 17' 1", is 192 sq. ft.; its terrace,
roughly 425 sq. ft. Although the floor space of the living room is
much greater than that of its two terraces, the total space of all the
rooms, about 2885 sq. ft., is not much more than that of all six terraces, about 2445 sq. ft.

OPPOSITE: *60. Stairs to second story.* ABOVE: *61. Guest bedroom in main house.* RIGHT: *62. Second-story landing, looking east.*

63. Second-story landing, looking west.

furniture supplier in Pittsburgh about fabricating a steel-frame "slumber bus," but without any results. The master bedroom, which gave freely onto the largest terrace, was graced with the most beautifully detailed fireplace: three large stones played upon the theme of ledge and cantilever and, at the other side, the stones were stepped-in as a reflex, in plan, of the cascade in the west-balcony staircase [66]. In the two west bedrooms the fireplaces were rather simple [67]. When an unusually reddish-colored stone slab more than 40 inches in breadth was discovered during the quarrying, it was used

to form a distinctive mantel over the third-story fireplace [68].

For the bathrooms, Edgar Kaufmann, jr., suggested floor and wall surfaces of cork—a softer, warmer and more textured material than ceramic tile. The corners, whether convex or concave, were to be curved to express Wright's ideals of plasticity and continuity [69]. The revised layouts for the bathrooms were finished on May 24. Mosher remembers what difficulties he had in convincing the contractor to execute the curved surfaces; he finally called out representatives of the Armstrong Cork

64. Bridge across drive.

Products Company, from Lancaster, Pennsylvania. He also remembers E. J. Kaufmann saying that, because the house was to be so indigenous to its site, perhaps the bathroom fixtures should be carved from the native rock; the thought of tubs, basins and stools sculptured from the dense sandstone still brings a smile to Mosher's ruddy face. This same concern of Kaufmann's, however, had resulted in the boulder being left untouched at the hearth. At the time, Mosher was not at all sure what he should do; then he decided to interview the nearest gravestone carvers. When Kaufmann went down to Bear Run the next weekend, Mosher had only to compare the cost of ordinary fixtures to the estimates from the carvers, and Kaufmann spoke no more about "indigenous" bathrooms [70].[13]

The kitchen was fitted with St. Charles cabinets and an

[13] The fixtures were supplied by Kohler of Kohler, Wis. Most of the toilet bowls are only 10½″ above the floor, and thus strangely sympathetic to the horizontal character of the house. They were sunk into hollows in the concrete floor slabs at the direction of Kaufmann, who subscribed to a health fad of the time favoring lower bowls as more "natural." In the later 1930s, Kohler even began to produce a 10″ bowl.

65. *Fallingwater from hill.*

66. Master-bedroom fireplace, November 1937.

AGA stove, neither being intended as in any way an expression of the special character of the house [71]. But the millwork and furniture, elsewhere, were to be. Wright wanted them to be in black-walnut plywood of "ship" quality, to resist warping from the humidity of the falls, and he recommended the Gillen Woodwork Corporation of Milwaukee as the best woodworking concern in the Middle West, though by no means the cheapest. Typically, the millwork contract would be a substantial part of the construction costs; Gillen's bid on June 4 came to about 4500 dollars. Edgar Tafel wrote Kaufmann that Gillen had worked on other of Wright's houses, including those for F. C. Robie and Darwin D. Martin, some 30 years earlier. George E. Gillen had been a vice-president of Matthews Bros. Manufacturing Company, which had done the millwork in major buildings all across the coun-

try. When the company was sold at auction early in 1937, he reorganized the plant with many of the same artisans —among them, Tony Prochaska, a Viennese, who was assigned the task of matching the veneers for the house on Bear Run.[14]

Kaufmann let the contract to Gillen on June 16. Tafel went up from Racine to Milwaukee on June 24 and visited the plant on North Port Washington Road to choose the flitches. Wright, too, visited the plant. Arthur Cooley, one of the cabinetmakers, spoke of Wright not long ago as an "eccentric," and recalled how he would appear in the shop with a cane and a floppy hat. Mosher remem-

[14] See the *Milwaukee Sentinel,* July 18, 1937, sec. B, pp. 7, 9. Gillen also did the millwork for Wright's house for Herbert F. Johnson, jr., north of Racine, Wis., as noted in *An Autobiography,* p. 477. Gillen went out of business in September 1941.

67. *Second-story west bedroom.*

bers that some of the cabinetmakers wanted to reject sap-wood from the veneers, but Wright liked the streaks and wanted them to run horizontally as a small-scale reiteration of the basic rhythm of the house. Most of the mill-work was shipped from Milwaukee in July and August.

Wright loved wood as "the most humanly intimate of all materials"; he accepted veneer as a means toward continuity, toward maintaining "the same flower of the grain over entire series or groups . . . as a unit."[15] Gillen's contract comprised doors, cabinets, wardrobes, backboards for beds, built-in seats and desks, radiator casings, tables and shelves. Edgar Kaufmann, jr., worked

[15] Wright, "The Meaning of Materials—Wood," *Architectural Record,* 63 (May 1928), pp. 481, 485.

on some of the details, including a system of sliding trays for linens. The trays were of walnut-framed cane, perforated for ventilation to avert mildew [72]. When the Kaufmanns noticed that much of the desk-top area in the two west bedrooms would be sacrificed to the radiator casings, Wright redesigned the desks so the tops would extend to the windows, with quarter-circles cut out to accommodate the inward swing of the casements [73]. Three small wood shelves at the head of the bed in Kaufmann's room picked up the rhythm of the quarter-circles.

For the seat and back cushions in the house, Edgar Kaufmann, jr., suggested "Dunlopillo," a vulcanized liquid latex honeycombed with air bubbles, which had been introduced in hospitals and for seating in such public facilities as theaters, hotels and churches. As a

LEFT: 68. *Third-story fireplace.* BE-
LOW LEFT: 69. *Bathroom surfaces
in cork.* BELOW RIGHT: 70. *Bathroom fixtures.*

71. The kitchen.

cushioning material, it was long-lasting and well ventilated. The built-in seats, which ran for more than 38 feet
along three sides of the living room, were the first to be
fitted with the cushions, supplied from the Dunlop Tire
& Rubber Company of Buffalo, New York. Mosher can
recall making rough sketches for some of the stools and
sending them to Wright for his correction and approval;
some of them were covered in bright red and yellow fab-
rics to serve as accents toward the middle of the room,

giving it a more intimate scale [74].

As the house was being furnished, at the end of October, both Wright and Kaufmann were aware that the
total costs were already about 70,000 dollars, or more
than twice what Kaufmann had intended to spend at
Bear Run. Wright wrote on October 25 to beg for more
money; he admitted that maintaining Taliesin was a
great extravagance, but he told Kaufmann that he had
gotten his money's worth from an architect, if ever a man

did. Wright said that if he ever again had to put so much of himself into a single commission, Taliesin would surely go out of business. He seemed able to summon his best rhetoric when short of money.

Wright continued to design more elaborate furnishings for the living room, and Kaufmann continued to resist what he considered to be too much formality. (Wright already was in control of much of the detail of the room, with the built-in seats, the dining table and its extensions, the desk near the hatch and, eventually, the six double-cushioned stools, six pedestal stools, four small square-topped tables and two coffee tables.) Kaufmann rejected his plan for specially patterned rugs, one of which would have been cut to fit around the boulder at the hearth; rejected four heavily ornamental incandescent floor lamps intended to cast light on the ceiling, and also a severely plain kind of fluorescent floor lamp, after trying both types; and rejected a set of circular chairs for the dining table, after trying one of them [75].[16] The dining table was equipped instead with six rather baroque chairs which Mrs. Kaufmann had bought in Florence; they at least offered the advantage of being three-legged and thus always stable on the irregular surfaces of the flag floor [76]. From the old Aladdin cabin the Kaufmanns brought in a few chairs to use in the kitchen and a few small cocktail tables, which were merely the inverted stumps of some of the dead chestnut trees. Mosher remembers that Wright did not like them, because the trees seemed to be growing in the wrong direction.

In the fall of 1937 the Kaufmanns began to use the house. They were visited very soon by John McAndrew, the new curator of architecture and industrial art at The Museum of Modern Art, in New York. He had left a teaching position at Vassar College; one of his students there had been Aline Bernstein, who was graduated in 1935; she and her brother, Charles Alan, a stage designer in New York, were related to Henry Kaufmann's wife;

[16] One of the tub chairs is now in the guest bedroom. Wright used an earlier, more monumental, version of this chair in his house of 1904–1905 for Darwin D. Martin, in Buffalo, N.Y. The 1930s version appeared in the Johnson house north of Racine, Wis.; cf. figs. 104 and 342 in Henry-Russell Hitchcock, *In the Nature of Materials* (New York, 1942). The impulse toward informality was shared by all the family, and Liliane Kaufmann was responsible for questioning the rugs, floor lamps, and dining chairs proposed by Wright for the main room. Her feeling was matched by her husband and son, and Edgar J. Kaufmann, as the client of record, naturally conveyed these ideas to Wright. It was Mrs. Kaufmann who first asked for a plunge pool (see p. 27) and for a way to reach it without passing through the living room (see p. 34). It was Wright who decided how these requests might best be fulfilled.

ABOVE: *72. Walnut wardrobe detail.* BELOW: *73. Bedroom desk detail.*

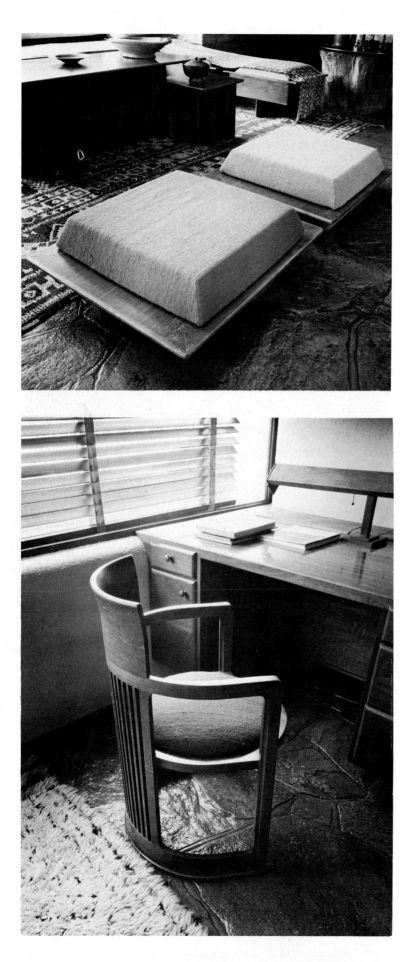

and that was how McAndrew got wind of the house on Bear Run:

> I had heard from Charles Alan who had heard from "Uncle Henry" that the Kaufmanns had got Mr. Wright to build them a strange week-end house. I wrote the Kaufmanns and asked whether it would be possible for me to see it on the way back from Chicago to New York . . . and got back an extraordinarily nice letter from Mrs. Kaufmann explaining that Bear Run was not in Pittsburgh but out in the country, and that the only way to see it would be to go for the weekend . . . .[17]

McAndrew remembers Mrs. Kaufmann telling him that he was the first person from the outside world to see the house. He was so impressed by what he saw that he soon planned a photographic exhibition of the house at The Museum of Modern Art.[18]

[17] John McAndrew, Boston. Letter of Dec. 15, 1975. [McAndrew died in February 1978 in Venice.]

[18] As an art critic for the *New York Times*, Aline Bernstein Louchheim illustrated Fallingwater ("Frank Lloyd Wright Talks of His Art," *New York Times Magazine*, Oct. 4, 1953, p. 27) and quoted Wright as saying: "We looked at the site of Bear Run, Pa., in 1936 [*sic*] and went home and made a drawing, and the building is almost exactly like it: Bear Run shows that buildings grow from their sites . . . ." Mrs. Louchheim was married to the architect Eero Saarinen later in 1953. McAndrew had not met Edgar Kaufmann, jr., before they drove to Bear Run together; later, he asked him to join the staff of the museum, and Kaufmann was an active force there in the design department for many years. He resigned in 1955.

ABOVE: *74. Cushioned stools in living room.* BELOW: *75. Circular chair.*

76. Dining-table chairs.

Chapter V
THE GUEST WING AND AFTER

Fallingwater entered the public imagination all at once, in January 1938. Early that month, the *Architectural Forum* gave its entire issue to Wright's work: Fallingwater took 12 pages, and Kaufmann's office in the store [77, 78] took two.[1] Wright designed the issue and provided the text. "The ideas involved here are in no wise changed from those of early work," he wrote of the house on Bear Run. "The materials and methods of construction come through them, here, as they may and will always come through everywhere. That is all. The effects you see in this house are not superficial effects." He chose to omit a concluding phrase he had written previously—"and are entirely consistent with the prairie houses of 1901–10."[2]

Wright was trying to say that the house did not result from any belated discovery on his part of modernist European architecture; that it flowered, rather, from his own principles and his own creativity, both of which had matured already some three decades earlier. Later, he referred to his house for Mrs. Thomas H. Gale, built about 1909, as the "progenitor as to general type" of Fallingwater.[3] He had John H. Howe restore an old perspective drawing of the Gale house and add to it the title "Oak Park 1904," along with the indication of a roof

trellis to the east, a detail which did not in fact exist, either in the original drawings or in the house as built. By "superficial effects" Wright meant the so-called International Style, which, he asserted, was two-dimensional, box-like and as inhibiting to spatial freedom as it was to any organic relationship with nature. The architects of that kind of modernism, he would write a few years later, were as much alike as peas in a pod: "All denying the pod though, and especially denying the vine on which the pod containing the peas grew."[4]

The portfolio of Wright's work in the *Forum* was intended to appeal to a public broader than the architectural profession; it was advertised on the inside front cover of *Life* magazine for January 17 with a dramatic photograph of Fallingwater from below the falls [79]. Wright mailed the cover to Kaufmann, saying that he was thrilled when he saw the picture, and that it surely meant a new era in architecture.

In his published commentary on the house, Wright saluted Kaufmann as an intelligent and appreciative client. George Nelson, who was then an editorial associate of the *Forum*, remembers working with Wright on the January issue:

> There is no doubt in my mind that for Wright the Kaufmann house was one of his great favorites, and I particularly remember the loving detail he would go into in describing how he developed the basic format and the details. For Wright, Edgar Kaufmann was one of his truly great and favorite clients, and as far as I am concerned, this high regard was well placed. Kaufmann was a true merchant prince, a man of great personal power, full of what we have come to call charisma and possessed of a vision that is anything but common. In

---

[1] The construction of the office had dragged on through the spring and summer of 1937. Built entirely of cypress hollow-core plywood supplied by the American Plywood Corporation of New London, Wis., it consisted of the floor and ceiling, a built-in seat, four chairs, five stools (ottomans), a long desk with extensions and built-in cabinets, the walls and louvers, and a mural that Edgar Kaufmann, jr., has described as "one of Wright's last architecturally sculptured walls." The dimensions of the room were about 26½ feet by 23 feet, with a ceiling height of eight feet. Sandoval had left the Fellowship and was living in Chicago; many years later he did the woodwork in Wright's shop for V. C. Morris, in San Francisco. Two carpets and the textiled upholstery for Kaufmann's office were handwoven in the studio of Loja Saarinen at Cranbrook, Bloomfield Hills, Mich., and were shipped to Pittsburgh on Jan. 3, 1938. Mrs. Saarinen was the daughter of the architect Herman Gesellius, wife of the architect Eliel Saarinen and mother of the architect Eero Saarinen.

[2] Cf. *Architectural Forum*, 68 (Jan. 1938), p. 36, and the ms. version as published in *Frank Lloyd Wright on Architecture*, ed. Frederick Gutheim (New York, 1941), p. 232.

[3] *Sixty Years of Living Architecture* (Los Angeles [1954?]), n.p.

[4] Wright, *An Autobiography*, p. 304. The notion of an International Style appeared in F. S. Onderdonk, *The Ferro-Concrete Style* (New York, 1928), before it was promoted at The Museum of Modern Art in New York. Le Corbusier toured America in the fall of 1935, and a small exhibition of his work was held at that museum. Walter Gropius and Ludwig Mies van der Rohe moved to America in 1937. A common, and annoying, reaction to Fallingwater was that Wright had at last "caught up" with the leading European modernists.

77. *Kaufmann's office in November 1937, before carpets and textiles were woven to Wright's designs by Loja Saarinen.*

retrospect, I would say that they did very well by each other.[5]

The house on Bear Run also appeared in the January 17 issue of *Time* magazine, both in a photograph and in the color rendering [see 19] which formed the background for a photograph of Wright, on the cover. *Time* called the house Wright's "most beautiful" work.[6]

John McAndrew's exhibition, "A New House on Bear Run, Penn., by Frank Lloyd Wright," opened January 24 in the museum's temporary quarters in the underground concourse of the former Time-Life Building, at 14 West Forty-ninth Street. It was composed of 20 photographs of

the house, and was accompanied by a brief catalogue which reproduced some of them, along with the plans and elevations and the same commentary by Wright as in the *Forum*.[7] Some of the early photographs of the house

[7] The exhibit ran until March 1. The photographs were by Hedrich-Blessing of Chicago (taken in November 1937), by Luke Swank of Pittsburgh (a friend of the Kaufmanns') and by McAndrew. Edward Alden Jewell reviewed the exhibit in the *New York Times* the day after it opened. Some of Swank's photos appeared in the *Pittsburgh Post-Gazette* on January 18 and in the magazine of the *Pittsburgh Press* on February 6. The *Art Digest* of February 1 mentioned both the exhibit and the special issue of the *Architectural Forum*, and on February 6 the gravure section of the *New York Herald-Tribune* published three of Hedrich-Blessing's photos. Lewis Mumford discussed the exhibit in *The New Yorker* of February 12, and Talbot F. Hamlin discussed and illustrated the house in the March issue of *Pencil Points*.

[5] George Nelson, New York. Letter of Dec. 31, 1973.
[6] *Time*, Jan. 17, 1938, p. 31.

78. *Opposite side of office, November 1937.*

show bare incandescent bulbs in the ceiling recesses of the living room [80]. Wright planned to conceal the lights behind panels of Japanese rice paper (which he was to buy in Chicago), as in shoji screens; some of his drawings for the more elaborate furnishing of the living room show that he was working within a pattern of floor modules two feet square and three feet square, rather like the traditional Japanese use of the tatami mat as a floor module. Wright wanted Gillen to make the ceiling panels, but their bid came to 714 dollars—which Kaufmann thought (and rightly) to be excessive. Kaufmann gave the order to a Pittsburgh mill, and although Wright had objected that no client had the right to go over his architect's head, he admitted later that Gillen had added onto the bid to compensate for the loss he had taken on

the rest of the millwork. Some of the framing members of the panels were sparingly ornamented with dentil bands, and the panels were filled in with beige muslin rather than rice paper [81].

The old Porter cottage on the hill was soon to be demolished to make way for the guest wing, servants' quarters and carport. Wright started just as he had with the main house, from another topographical map, this one (dated January 22, 1938) focusing on the hill. Kaufmann sent him the map on January 25, along with these instructions:

In planning the servants' wing, the following will be the requirements: 4 single bed rooms for servants, one bath. If possible, a combination kitchen, laundry and sitting room . . . when there is no cooking and no laundry, the

ABOVE: 79. *Fallingwater, November 1937.* OPPOSITE ABOVE: 80. *Central recess in living-room ceiling, November 1937.* OPPOSITE BELOW: 81. *Ceiling recess paneled.*

room could be used as a sitting room for the servants. There should be a minimum space allowed for four cars to be stored, and we should like, if possible, to add two single and one double guest rooms and bath.

The plans and elevations were finished by May 2, but the Kaufmanns found them unsatisfactory. All the guest rooms gave onto a gallery along the north side; one basic objection went to the lack of cross-ventilation. The entrance to the guest wing would have been unusually frontal and formal, and the connection to the main house entailed an enclosed pedestrian bridge from the third-story level which would have extended for 39 feet to form an awkward, monotonous and tunnel-like passage to a semicircular covered walkway. The entire scheme, in short, was strangely without Wright's usual subtlety.

Between the spring and fall of 1938, for only 18,000 dollars, the architect Walter Gropius built a house for himself in Lincoln, Massachusetts, without a single specially designed part. Edgar Kaufmann, jr., was surprised to find better hardware from Hope's than had been supplied to Bear Run.[8] He complained to Hope's, and between October 25 and December 2 ten sheets of drawings were made for revisions to the hardware of the double folding-out doors to the terraces, the single side-hung doors, the casement screen doors and so on. Nine more sheets were finished by January 14, 1939. Most of the screens were yet to be made. When they arrived, Edgar Kaufmann, jr., suggested that they be left in the factory finish, a blue-gray, for contrast with the Cherokee red of the steel sash.

When the plans for the guest wing and servants' quarters were finally rejected by Kaufmann, Wright quickly mailed a set of revised drawings. Thumm passed them on to the Metzger-Richardson Company by the middle of January 1939 for a review of the structural details. Foundation work was begun by the first of February, but for the next three months Wright continued to make changes in the plans, much to Thumm's exasperation: room dimensions, window sizes, slab overhangs and the placement of furniture were all changed, Thumm complained to Kaufmann on March 1. Each drawing that came from Wright, he said, represented "a change over the previous drawing . . . . Willingly I have spent considerable time trying to properly decipher the architectural intent and thereby furnish Hall with the necessary field interpretation and dimensions . . . ." The engineers had given up twice in trying to figure the structural members, Thumm

[8] Hope's advertised in the Jan. 1938 *Architectural Forum*, p. 21, with a photograph of the corner drop-out windows: "The manufacture of this combination of steel casement windows, and of the many others which form such attractive details in the residence, called for special construction in our shops."

wrote. The amount of heat radiation as indicated on Wright's drawings was less than half of what was necessary. Millwork drawings sent to Gillen would have to be scrapped because Wright kept coming up with new layouts. In a second memorandum to Kaufmann, on March 7, Thumm worried that the electrical work might have to be changed and that a new drawing might be in error in showing a nine-foot overhang to the roof slab that projected from the carport. Wright soon wired that the cantilever was to be nine feet, as shown.

Wright had the "final" revised set of drawings ready by April 28. In the main house, meanwhile, Edgar Kaufmann, jr., was busy with changes to the lighting. He thought that fluorescent tubes, which were already in commercial use, might be used with baffles to create better indirect lighting, and so most of the lighting became fluorescent.

As the guest wing and servants' quarters were being finished, Wright again made a characteristic plea for more money. In a letter of September 2, he juggled some figures and estimates and asserted that Kaufmann owed him a balance of more than 4200 dollars. Wright wrote that Kaufmann had paid him all that he had asked for, but he had not asked for enough. Wright said he was not asking for justice but for mercy. In anticipation of a few further services, Wright asked Kaufmann to send him a final payment of 5000 dollars, in two installments. Kaufmann responded on September 14:

I sent you a telegram today telling you a check was going forward, but for your information your figuring is all cock-eyed. Although we have made complete settlement on the original house, the office and the guest wing, I still feel that your request is reasonable . . . .

The scheme for the guest wing was reduced from the original plans but was hardly impoverished [82]. The narrow drive behind the main house doubled back in climbing the hill and passed through massive stone terminals to enter a gravel court planned, clearly, on a 30–60 triangle. The four stalls for cars were separated by stone piers canted at the 30-degree angle, and all were screened at the south by the chauffeur's room [83]. On the second story were two single servants' rooms and a double room which opened onto a terrace above the north end of the carport. Although the servants' rooms were small and simple and served only by a single bathroom, they were finished as if bedrooms in the main house.

A slight rise in elevation, a recessed stair space [see 59] and a stone chimney which rose 18½ feet separated the guest wing from the carport. It consisted simply of a "guest lounge," or living room [84], and a bedroom [85]. Between the two were a bathroom (lighted and

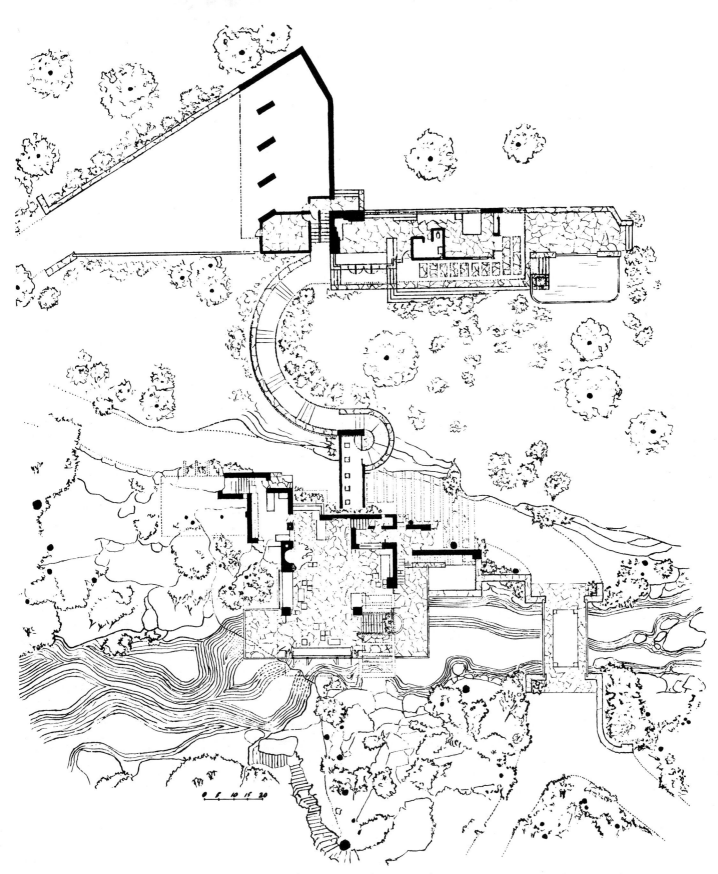

82. Plan of guest-wing connection.

OPPOSITE ABOVE: 83. *Carports and servants' quarters.* OPPOSITE BELOW: 84. *Guest lounge.* ABOVE: 85. *Guest bedroom.* LEFT: 86. *Fireplace in guest lounge.*

ventilated by a monitor roof with clerestories on three sides), a short gallery lined with wardrobes and a short entry hall cut from the space of the lounge by an open screen of wooden framing members. The lounge was 23 feet long, a simple space, warm and restful, with built-in seating along the south bank of windows (the cushions three feet wide, to serve as extra beds), and an especially beautiful fireplace formed of unusually broad stones, striated and thus a revelation of the native sedimentary beds [86]. The mantel was a stone six feet long. In plan, the fireplace was stepped-in much like that in the master bedroom of the main house. Again the step motif would appear close by in profile, this time in the staircasing to the second-story rooms of the servants' quarters. Although the guest bedroom was of modest size (about 13 feet north-south and 15 feet eight inches east-west) it opened through glass doors to a swimming pool—at long last—about 31 feet long [87]. At first, in the heat of summer, Mrs. Kaufmann favored the guest wing over the main house. She enjoyed the pool and the greater seclusion, and, indoors, the cross-ventilation from the clerestory which ran continuously along the north wall.

Addressed southeastward, on axis with the main house, the guest wing faced a long terrace sheltered by a roof slab cantilevered about seven feet past the wall [88].

Near the corner, the slab changed into another trellis through a series of openings between beams spaced 40 inches apart [89]. William Wesley Peters remembers making the structural calculations for the slab (seven inches thick, or about the same as in the parapets of the main house). It hovered only six feet four and one-half inches above the terrace.[9] But the slab was folded upward at the line of windows, to create a ceiling indoors of more than seven feet nine inches. The fold expanded the living space, strengthened the cantilever, expressed structural continuity and formed an upper wall face, outdoors, which echoed the long planes of the parapets in the main house.

Wright might have easily sited the guest wing somewhere off in the woods, and even hidden it entirely from the main house, so it would have been obliged to reflect the character of the main house only in a relaxed way. But the privacy of both residences was already guaranteed by a marked difference in elevation (more than 60 feet from the piers beneath the bolsters to the top of the guest-lounge chimney) and by distance (more than 90 feet). So he faced head-on the challenge of joining

[9] The lowest ceiling in the main house occurs in the third-story gallery; at certain points it is now only 6′ 3¾″, although it was supposed to be 6′ 4½″.

OPPOSITE: *87. Swimming pool.*
LEFT: *88. Terrace by guest wing.*
BELOW: *89. Trellis by guest bedroom.*

them, to make the wing clearly a dependency of the main house [90]. This he accomplished with a masterly stroke as graceful as it was daring: the covered walkway, a kind of gallery, which swooped down from the guest-wing terrace to the cliff above the driveway, returned on itself in a separate and reflex semicircle, then entered a much shorter bridgeway (a span of only 17 feet) to the main house, joining it at the second story rather than at the third [91, 92]. When this grand connection is perceived as a system of arcs—the larger arc is swung on an outside radius of 28 feet, and its reflex on an inside radius of seven and one-half feet—the covered walkway becomes the culmination of all the curved surfaces in the house. A circular stone planter at the juncture of the bridgeway and the reflex of the canopy, in which a moss garden [93] grows half indoors and half out, by creeping under a pane of glass, becomes a period to the entire composition.[10]

[10] Another moss garden, entirely outdoors, is at the east end of the landing north of the guest terrace. Planters for flowers and cuttings of rhododendron are at the south corners of the living room, at the east end of the hatch, at diagonally opposite terminals of the bridge over the stream, at the wall between the bridge and the loggia, in the metal "newel" at the second-story stair landing, on the third-story terrace (to conceal the vents from the guest bathroom below) and by the guest-wing swimming pool.

90. *Fallingwater in the forest.*

The canopy above the walkway manifested every essential element of the house. It was cantilevered broadly; the slab was folded for strength and in continuity; and it cascaded from the hill, tripping and spilling, as one last allusion to the falling stream. Mosher remembers asking Wright how the canopy could possibly be supported by the steel posts only at its circumference; for an answer, he says, Wright raised his forearm and hand to demonstrate how difficult it was, so long as the hand remained flat, to pull the hand below a line forming a right angle with the forearm. Peters again had to make the actual calculations. The canopy slab was eight feet wide but only three and one-half inches thick, and it acted somewhat as a ring beam, with a system of steel reinforcement composed of half-inch bars running circumferentially, square bars one and one-eighth inches thick, three-eighths-inch bars and three-fourths-inch straight bars: a veritable weaving of steel in tension, to form the kind of structure Wright liked to compare with a spider's web.

For the main canopy, there were five steel posts, which varied as the canopy stepped downward, from almost seven feet high to less than four feet. Each post was composed of two welded angle members (three-fourths-inch plate, three and one-half inches on each side). The main canopy reached from the roof of the guest wing to the parapet of the bridgeway; the small reflex canopy required only a single supporting post, a sort of dwarf column only 23 inches high. Another terrace was created by paving the roof of the bridgeway with flags. Inside, the bridgeway was lighted by a row of five skylights, each sized the same as the lights built into the floor of the bridge across the stream (15 inches square); the skylights were fitted with incandescent bulbs to serve also as night lights. At the north end of the bridgeway, near the moss garden, a boulder was allowed to penetrate the structure [94].

Steel flanges were welded to the posts which supported the canopy. They introduced a distinct ornamental motif, a jagged profile repeated every eight inches, which expressed how the columns transferred the weight of the canopy into the stone retaining wall of the walkway [95]. The finished columns were painted Cherokee red; the angular pattern of the flanges related to nothing else in the house except the light fixtures built into the trellis beams by the east living-room terrace [see 33], across the drive [see 36] and at the guest wing [see 89]—fixtures shaped like irregular pentagons (five inches along the top and three inches on each of the four sides) and also pointed downward. Were both these details allusions to Indians—the pointed lights to arrowheads, the flanges to feathering?[11]

True ornament, said Wright, was "the inherent melody of structure"; it should exist as the "manifest *abstract pattern of structure itself.*"[12] His ornamental range at Bear Run, often enough overlooked, was precisely that: the cantilevered metal shelves in the living room, the cantilevered wine sphere, the screens below the ceiling lights framed as if a miniature system of beams and joists, the cantilevered trellis beams, the cantilevered and rounded edges of the furniture, the rounded edges of the reinforced concrete, the rounded returns of the stair hangers, the rounded steps. Rarely had his ornament been so understated and so rigorously integrated with the fabric of the building itself.

Through 1939, while the guest wing and the covered walkway were being built, more changes were made in the hardware and lighting of the main house. Mosher's assignment to Bear Run at last came to an end, and he returned to Taliesin to help with the plans for the George Sturges house in California and the John Pew house in Wisconsin. Both were to have broadly cantilevered terraces.

As they settled into their new house, the Kaufmanns gradually introduced various works of art, indoors and out. Wright had given them a few Japanese prints from his own collection, but their tastes were rather more catholic than his, and the house proved more than accommodating. Edgar Kaufmann, jr., once wrote that Wright on his later visits to Bear Run never made a sarcastic remark about the modernist sculptures, although he "would invariably ask to have new statues relocated, often only a few feet from where they were . . . directing the sculpture into a telling position where it accentuated a feature of the architecture, and in turn gained the support of its setting."[13]

[11] Wright's interest in Indian motifs dated from the 1890s, when, as Edgar Kaufmann, jr., has observed, he was already fond of the sculptures of Hermon A. MacNeil (1866–1947), who adopted Indians as his subject matter after seeing them perform at the World's Columbian Exposition of 1893. Wright's 1922 projects for the Tahoe Summer Colony were inspired by a wigwam motif. He designed his own sculptures of Indians for his 1924 project for the Nakoma Country Club, which he frankly called an "Indianesque affair." He also called the living space of the Johnson house near Racine the "wigwam." Lloyd Wright said in 1971 that he and his father had sought continuity with the work of the Indians of the Southwest and of Pre-Columbian Mexico and Mesoamerica. See David Gebhard and Harriette Von Breton, *Lloyd Wright, Architect* (Santa Barbara, Calif., 1971), p. 72. Edgar Kaufmann, jr., is not convinced that the two details of Fallingwater allude to Indians, and he is even less sympathetic to the notion advanced by Vincent Scully, jr., in "Wright vs. the International Style," *Art News,* 53 (March 1954), p. 65, that the house is Mayan-like in its massing.

[12] *Frank Lloyd Wright on Architecture,* ed. Frederick Gutheim (New York, 1941), p. 236, and *An Autobiography,* p. 347 (his italics).

[13] Edgar Kaufmann, jr., "The Fine Arts and Frank Lloyd Wright," in *Four Great Makers of Modern Architecture* (New York, 1963), p. 35.

RIGHT: *91. Canopy above walkway
from guest wing to main house.*
BELOW: *92. Return of canopy.*
OPPOSITE ABOVE: *93. Moss garden.*
OPPOSITE BELOW: *94. Boulder in
bridgeway.*

95. *Steel-post detail.*

After 1939, few changes were made to the house or guest wing. Because the bridgeway over the drive had been shifted from the third story of the main house to the second, the gallery (more than 26 feet long) became only a vestigial passage leading nowhere; but Edgar Kaufmann, jr., adopted the small space east of the stairwell as his bedroom [96]. This cheerful nook caught the early morning light and opened conveniently to the third-story terrace (which was nearly 34 feet long). Thus the west bedroom of the third story became his study, a quiet space which led by way of the small west balcony down to his father's terrace.

Engineering reports on the deflections continued at regular intervals: the third report, submitted in May 1940, took note of "a further settlement of one quarter of an inch," but found the structure to be in "very good condition." Some of the hanger bars in the steps to the stream were found bent, but it was assumed that the stress came only from heavy snow loads.

V. M. Bearer, the district forester who had inspected Bear Run in. 1932, returned in September 1940. In a report dated the 17th, he suggested that black-walnut seedlings be planted in the occasional openings of the forest where charcoal hearths once had been operated. Bearer was pleased by what he saw at Bear Run, and his pleasure must have been Kaufmann's too. "It is, indeed, gratifying to learn that my recommendations made eight years ago have been followed," Bearer wrote. "The area is well stocked with mixed hardwoods, laurel, rhododendron, hemlock and many shrubs. The clear, cold water of the swift and rocky Bear Run . . . helps make this one of the finest areas in Pennsylvania."

In the years of World War II, the Kaufmanns began wintering in California. By 1944, while Edgar Kaufmann, jr., was serving in the Army Air Force, they were planning a new house at 470 West Vista de Chino, in Palm Springs. Their architect was not Wright, but Richard Neutra of Los Angeles. When he returned from the service and first saw the blueprints, Edgar Kaufmann, jr., was outraged; a few years later, about 1950, he asked Wright to design him a house for a site adjacent to his father's house. Wright planned a magnificent residence with walls of desert boulders (boulders were scattered all about the well-clipped lawn of the house planned by Neutra), arranged in segments of circles and their reflexes. The house of boulders was never built, and perhaps the commission was more nearly intended as a chance for Wright to show what he might have done had E. J. Kaufmann not gone to Neutra: the difference, that is, between "organic" architecture and the International Style, or what Neutra chose to call his "biorealism."[14]

In 1946, the elder Kaufmann planned to extend the kitchen of the house on Bear Run into a sitting room for

96. Third-story gallery.

14 For a plan and two color renderings of the house of boulders see *Frank Lloyd Wright: Sixty Years of Living Architecture,* ed. Werner Moser (Winterthur, Switz., 1952), pp. 96–97. Richard Neutra (1892–1970), a Viennese architect, came to America in 1923; he met Wright in April 1924 at the funeral of Louis Sullivan, and soon spent several months at Taliesin. In 1925 he began sharing a studio in Los Angeles with R. M. Schindler (1887–1953), another Viennese, who had come to America in 1914 and had worked with Wright from 1918 to 1922. In 1932 Wright saw his own work exhibited between that of Neutra and Schindler at the University of California at Los Angeles, and he thought of Christ being crucified between two thieves. For the Kaufmann house in Palm Springs, see *Richard Neutra: 1923–50,* ed. W. Boesiger (New York, 1964), pp. 71–79, or Richard Neutra, *Mystery and Realities of the Site* (Scarsdale, N.Y., 1951), pp. 32–39. In a lecture at the University of Kansas on March 13, 1963, Neutra said of his Kaufmann house: "This is a house that is partaking of the dynamic changes around it . . . . This building is changing. It is oriented into [*sic*] the landscape. It is underlining, with its simple geometric forms, the ruggedness of the mountain-scape."

the servants, without mentioning the addition to Wright; but his son prevailed, and Wright was consulted. The original kitchen, which measured only 15½ feet by 12 feet two inches, was the only space in the house of rather ordinary quality. Beginning in June, part of the stone wall under the west-bedroom terrace was removed and a new wall was built to provide for the addition; the drawings were finished on July 26, and the new space, which measured nine feet six inches by ten feet seven inches, became an inconspicuous room with a mitred-glass window at the salient south corner, a large casement window also at the south, and a slit window at the west corner which gave an unexpected view of the boulder beneath the west terrace. The slit window had the character of one of Wright's touches, but the lack of articulation and the broad expanse of the other windows noticeably did not [97].

In July and August there were also drawings for installing a heater room in the guest wing; the heat previously had been pumped from the system of the main house—forced hot water from an oil-fired furnace supplied by H. A. Thrush & Company of Peru, Indiana.

Although they usually entertained only a few guests,

the Kaufmanns occasionally found the house too cramped in two places, the entry alcove and the dining area. And so, late in 1947—some questions were discussed in October, and another site plan was prepared in November—Wright began to design an entirely new entrance scheme which would extend the house into the driveway, in order to enlarge the dining space, and which would add what he called the "Shady Lane entrance," with another row of car stalls, higher on the hill above the guest wing. The plans came to nothing; indeed, they became the first of a long series of commissions from the Kaufmanns destined to result only in drawings. Wright was paid his fees, of course, and often generously—Kaufmann once sent him a new automobile as a Christmas gift, unannounced—but he found himself increasingly discouraged by what seemed a persistent pattern of suggestions and ideas doomed never to be realized. Wright by now was in his eighties; it was getting late, he wrote rather sadly, for him to be watching his best efforts going to waste, spent merely on sketches.

In 1947 and 1948, Kaufmann had Wright at work on vast and various schemes to redevelop the Point Park, in Pittsburgh, into a constellation of bridges, highways,

half inches, since the year before, in the roof above the guest-bedroom terrace of the main house. Roy M. Oliver, who had succeeded Thumm as superintendent of the store buildings and who was likewise obliged to attend to Bear Run, sent the report to Wright. In September, after an earlier attempt to jack the roof had merely depressed the floor, a post was inserted between the east end of the parapet and the sagging roof. Later, a row of five slender bars was added; they made the support look as if it had been designed. But a second post was installed in July 1953 in a much more obtrusive place on the south parapet, with a post beneath it resting on the plunge-pool stair wall. After further "signs of distress" were detected by the engineers, the east part of the roof was rebuilt, in September 1954. Wet insulation was found in the old slab, and the reinforcement bars were found to have been carelessly placed.

Kaufmann was still receiving reports from the engineers during the last weeks of his life. In a report of March 9, 1955, they said that the window glass near the stairwell to the stream had shattered, the mullions were no longer plumb and the doors from the living room to the east terrace did not open "readily." All were signs of progressive settlement, they said. Their conclusion was politely ominous: "we believe that for some years this structure has been quietly asking for help (by bending stair hangers, twisting frames, and breaking glass) and that in the near future it will demand assistance in a more forceful manner."

Kaufmann had been in ill health. He died at his Palm Springs home on April 15, only a few hours after Wright had visited him.[16] Their long association had hardly been free of conflicts and worries, but Kaufmann relished their times together and he knew very well the value of what they had brought into being. For his part, Wright once told Kaufmann that their friendship had gone quite

towers and civic facilities such as theaters, an aquarium and—strangely reminiscent of their earliest discussions, back in 1934—a planetarium. In 1949 and 1950, Kaufmann had him design two versions of a self-service parking garage; it, too, would have been a structure of continuously coiling ramps in reinforced concrete and would have connected with the store (which had been merged with the May Company, of New York, in October 1946) from the Fourth Avenue side. There was the project for the Palm Springs house of boulders and, in 1952, a project for a "Rhododendron Chapel," a place for meditation, on the Bear Run grounds. (Wright's design for the chapel was overscaled, suggesting a place for services; with its faceted roof of glass it was even slightly reminiscent of his project in 1926 for a great steel cathedral—"for a million people"—in New York.) Wright in 1952 and 1953 designed for Kaufmann two versions of a "Point View" apartment tower for a site in Pittsburgh, and in 1957 he made plans for a gate lodge, television-antenna tower and swimming pool at Bear Run.[15]

Through the years, except during World War II, engineering firms continued to take sightings of the house on Bear Run to check for further deflections, and a reading of May 27, 1950, showed a settlement of about one and a

[15] For illustrations of the unexecuted projects: new entrance scheme and burial chapel, *Frank Lloyd Wright: Drawings for a Living Architecture* (New York, 1959), pp. 91, 92; Pittsburgh Point Park, *Taliesin Drawings* (New York, 1952), pp. 46–51, and *The Drawings of Frank Lloyd Wright* (New York, 1962), figs. 228–230, 277; parking garage, *Taliesin Drawings*, pp. 56–57, and *The Drawings of Frank Lloyd Wright*, figs. 226 and 227; and Point View Apartments, *ibid.*, figs. 247 and 248.

[16] See the *Pittsburgh Post-Gazette*, April 16, 1955, pp. 1, 4–5. After the May Company named a new president for Kaufmann's Store, the office was dismantled; in 1956, Edgar Kaufmann, jr., had it reinstalled on the fifteenth floor of the First National Bank Building in Pittsburgh to serve the offices of the Edgar J. Kaufmann Charitable Foundation and Charitable Trust. Later, the office was dismantled again. In 1974, Edgar Kaufmann, jr., gave it to the Victoria and Albert Museum in South Kensington, London, where it was first exhibited from Oct. 19 to Nov. 15 of that year. Eventually the office will be installed in the projected twentieth-century primary galleries. See Toni del Renzio, "Frank Lloyd Wright & The Pop Traditions," *Art & Artists* (London), 9 (Jan. 1975), pp. 3, 28 ff.

beyond the ordinary relationship of architect to client, and that the result had been Fallingwater. Mrs. Kaufmann, who died on September 7, 1952, had once sent Wright a birthday greeting in which she wrote: "Living in a house built by you has been my one education . . . ."[17]

Now it was up to Edgar Kaufmann, jr., to protect the house from the drastic measures of structural reinforcement so predictably proposed by the engineers. In the summer of 1955 he had plans made for strengthening the stairs from the hatch; two steel angle bars were carried down into the bedrock of the stream and were placed closer to the original ties to the bedrock (doubled T-bars, welded back to back) so the two hangers of the bottom tread could be eliminated. The change was slight and was executed with great care [98].

A flood in the fall of 1954 had damaged the stairs, but a much more severe storm and flood assaulted the house in August 1956, as Edgar Kaufmann, jr., has recalled:

> Water rose far above the living room floor, and although the terrace doors kept most of it out, the bridge to the guest wing was more leaky. The stairs became a cascade. The wind was violent and of course all wires were down. Worse, the house was hung with pendant scaffoldings of heavy timber, as we had begun to repaint. The scaffolding was caught in the wind and shook the whole house like a terrier shakes a rat. I was there (it was a week-end) and felt sure that somewhere something must snap. To release the scaffolding was impossible, its nails were tightly gripped by the water-soaked timbers. There was nothing to do but pile up the furniture and wait. In four or five hours the storm

abated. The damage to the property was enormous; to the house, nil; only much cleaning of mud and sand was required.[18]

Frank Lloyd Wright's last book, *A Testament*, was published in 1957. In it he mentioned Fallingwater as his first dwelling in reinforced concrete, and one which established a new grammar true to the material. He died on April 9, 1959, in Phoenix, at nearly 92 years old.

For several more years, Edgar Kaufmann, jr., continued to use the house on Bear Run. In September 1963, he announced his intention of giving the house to the public in care of the Western Pennsylvania Conservancy, of Pittsburgh. The house and 1543 acres surrounding it were formally accepted in a ceremony on October 29 as "The Kaufmann Conservation on Bear Run, a Memorial to Edgar J. and Liliane S. Kaufmann."[19] That day, Edgar Kaufmann, jr., looked back on his years with the house:

> Its beauty remains fresh like that of the nature into which it fits. It has served well as a home, yet has always been more than that: a work of art, beyond any ordinary measures of excellence . . . . House and site together form the very image of man's desire to be at one with nature, equal and wedded to nature . . . . Such a place cannot be possessed. It is a work by man for man, not by a man for a man . . . . By its very intensity it is a public resource, not a private indulgence.

As a work of art, the house on Bear Run reveals itself slowly, and never once and for all [99, 100]. There was never any house quite like it before, and there has been none since.

[17] "My father Frank Lloyd Wright was always fond of the Kaufmann house, the site and the Kaufmanns and their co-operation," Lloyd Wright writes in a letter of March 27, 1974. "He recognized the house as a 'landmark' in his architectural creations, which indeed it has been. Father was always grateful for the interest and understanding support of the Kaufmanns, father and son." [Lloyd Wright died in May 1978 in California, at the age of 88.]

[18] Edgar Kaufmann, jr., "Twenty-five Years of the House on the Waterfall," *L'architettura—cronache e storia*, 82 (Aug. 1962), p. 42.

[19] Since then, the Conservancy has purchased 1120 more acres in an effort to safeguard the Bear Run watershed. As a private nonprofit organization founded in 1931, the Conservancy primarily seeks to acquire land especially suitable for state parks and nature reserves. The Kaufmann Conservation on Bear Run is supported by an endowment from the Edgar J. Kaufmann Charitable Foundation. Late in 1976, all the concrete surfaces of the house were sandblasted, repaired, resurfaced, painted and sealed. The house had been painted seven times prior to this major restoration.

99. *Fallingwater in winter.*

100. Fallingwater at dusk.

INDEX